Trends in
Organizational
Behavior

Volume 3

Trends in Organizational Behavior

Volume 3

Edited by

Cary L. Cooper

Manchester School of Management, University of Manchester Institute of
Science and Technology, UK

and

Denise M. Rousseau

Carnegie-Mellon University, Pittsburgh, USA

JOHN WILEY & SONS
Chichester · New York · Brisbane · Toronto · Singapore

Copyright © 1996 by John Wiley & Sons Ltd,
          Baffins Lane, Chichester,
          West Sussex PO19 1UD, England

          National   01243 779777
          International   (+44) 1243 779777
          e-mail (for orders and customer service enquiries): cs-books@wiley.co.uk
          Visit our Home Page on http://www.wiley.co.uk
                        or http://www.wiley.com

Trends in Organizational Behavior, Volume 3

Published as a supplement to the
Journal of Organizational Behavior, Volume 17

Other Wiley Editorial Offices

John Wiley & Sons, Inc., 605 Third Avenue,
New York, NY 10158-0012, USA

Jacaranda Wiley Ltd, 33 Park Road, Milton,
Queensland 4064, Australia

John Wiley & Sons (Canada) Ltd, 22 Worcester Road,
Rexdale, Ontario M9W 1L1, Canada

John Wiley & Sons (Asia) Pte Ltd, 2 Clementi Loop #02-01,
Jin Xing Distripark, Singapore 129809

British Library Cataloguing in Publication data

A catalogue record for this book is available from the British Library

ISBN 0-471-96585-5

Typeset in 10/12pt Palatino by Mackreth Media Services, Hemel Hempstead, Herts
Printed and bound in Great Britain by Redwood Books, Trowbridge, Wiltshire
This book is printed on acid-free paper responsibly manufactured from sustainable forestation,
for which at least two trees are planted for each one used for paper production

Contents

About the Editors

CARY L. COOPER

Currently Professor of Organizational Psychology and Pro-Vice Chancellor at the University of Manchester Institute of Science and Technology, Professor Cooper is the author of over 80 books (on stress, women at work, and industrial and organizational psychology), has written over 250 articles for academic journals, and is a frequent contributor to national newspapers, TV, and radio. Founding President of the British Academy of Management, he is currently Editor-in-Chief of the *Journal of Organizational Behavior*, and a Fellow of the British Psychological Society, the Royal Society of Arts and the Royal Society of Medicine.

DENISE M. ROUSSEAU

Professor of Organization Behavior at Carnegie-Mellon University, Professor Rousseau received her doctorate in Industrial/Organizational Psychology from the University of California at Berkeley. Her research interests include psychological contracts, strategic human resource management, and organizational culture. Her research has appeared in prominent academic journals, such as *Journal of Applied Psychology*, *Academy of Management Review*, *Academy of Management Journal*, and *Administrative Science Quarterly*, and she is an author of the books *Developing an Interdisciplinary Science of Organizations* and *Psychological Contracts in Organizations*. She is a Fellow of both the American Psychological Association and the Society for Industrial/Organizational Psychology and is an Associate Editor of the *Journal of Organizational Behavior*.

Contributors

Julian Barling
Department of Psychology, Queen's University, Kingston, Ontario K7L 3N6, Canada.

Matthew C. Bloom
ILR School, Cornell University, 393 Ives Hall, Ithaca, New York 14583-3901, USA.

Beth Chung
Department of Psychology, University of Maryland, College Park, MD 20742, USA.

Eric D. Darr
Anderson Graduate School of Management, University of California, 110 Westwood Plaza, Box 951481, Los Angeles, CA 90095, USA.

Paul S. Goodman
Graduate School of Industrial Administration, Carnegie Mellon University, Pittsburgh, PA 15213, USA.

Liane Greenberg
Department of Psychology, Queen's University, Kingston, Ontario K7L 3N6, Canada.

Richard A. Guzzo
Department of Psychology, University of Maryland, College Park, MD 20742, USA.

Boris Kabanoff
Australian Graduate School of Management, University of New South Wales, PO Box 1, Kensington NSW 2033, Australia.

David Krackhardt
H. John Heinz III School of Public Policy and Management, Carnegie Mellon University, Pittsburgh, PA 15213, USA.

George T. Milkovich
ILR School, Cornell University, 393 Ives Hall, Ithaca, New York 14583-3901, USA.

Motohiro Morishima
Faculty of Policy Management, Keio University, 5322 Endo, Fujisawa, Kanagawa 252, Japan.

Benjamin Schneider
Department of Psychology, University of Maryland, College Park, MD 20742, USA.

Peter D. Sherer
Johnson Graduate School of Management, Cornell University, Ithaca, New York 14583-3901, USA.

Editorial Introduction

Trends, Volume 3 continues our practice of spotlighting innovations in organizational research. This year's *Trends* presents emerging topics from service quality and expatriates to organizational learning and employee theft. It also describes state-of-the-art organizational research methodologies from computer-aided text analysis to network studies. A striking feature of this volume's chapters is their emphasis on research that informs us regarding contemporary organizational problems. Our authors address the relevance of organizational research to such diverse concerns as corporate performance and competitive responsiveness, employee loyalty and relations to firms, and management in a global setting.

Boris Kabanoff leads off by describing how computers can aid our understanding of organizations and their performance by assisting in the analysis of organizational communiqués. Shareholder reports, press releases, and other communications give access to organizations' world views and provide insights regarding the organizational "black box", the cognitions and interpretations organizations possess regarding their environment and themselves. Matthew Bloom and George Milkovich probe issues surrounding contemporary managerial and executive compensation. Viewing compensation practices as a "bundle" of exchanges, they integrate the loosely knit theories and research on compensation into a coherent view which prompts consideration of the social contract surrounding compensation of highly paid executives. While employee loyalty and citizenship are typical contemporary concerns, Liane Greenberg and Julian Barling investigate the flip-side, describing current research regarding employee theft. Predispositions, workplace factors and increasingly dysfunctional employment relations are implicated in this significant phenomenon. Using a market segment typology, Benjamin Schneider and Beth Chung offer a contemporary way of thinking about the nature of service and the problems service delivery can create for the management of service businesses. Because many problems are due to the ways in which services differ from products, they place particular emphasis on these differences and their role in the service encounter. In tackling services marketing from an organizational perspective, Schneider and Chung challenge the boundary between the fields of organizational behavior and marketing. Paul Goodman and Eric Darr combine two contemporary topics, organizational learning and computer-mediated communication, in their treatment of a powerful application: computer-assisted learning systems (CALS). Organizations adopting CALS can reap benefits in terms of widely distributed innovations, adapted to local needs. But the factors that impede organizational learning also can hinder realization of CALS' benefits. Goodman and Darr provide insights into best practices and future research needs. Peter Scherer develops a new framework for understanding work arrangements, based on the diversity of work forms embodied in employment, contracts, and ownership. As firms differentiate in creating new capabilities they deploy labor in novel ways (e.g. leasing, contracting) which are not well understood in conventional theories of employment. Scherer presents alternative models of work arrangements and a grammar for building new theory. Richard Guzzo investigates the employment relationship of firms with their expatriate employees. Focusing on core areas of compensation practices, human capital investments, and employee well-being, Guzzo describes problems arising due to overseas assignments, and develops their implications for research. Motohiro Morishima challenges many assumptions researchers and managers make regarding Japanese employment contracts. Developing the concept of "flexible rigidities", Morishima specifies fundamental assumptions in Japanese work arrangements and the current stresses which might weaken these traditionally robust features of employment in Japanese corporations. Scenarios for the future are portrayed and assessed against contemporary workforce data, psychological contract theory, and the flexible rigidity Morishima sees at the core of Japanese work arrangements. In our last chapter, David Krackhardt employs the perspective and methodology of network analysis to gain insights into the problems new managers face when they assume responsibilities in a part of the organization in which they have no experience. Adopting the concept of "liability of newness" from macro Organizational Behavior research into the problems firms face when they come into existence, Krackhardt pursues its micro implications for managerial behavior and performance.

This third volume of *Trends* attempts, as have the others, to capture some of the scope and scale of contemporary organizational research. Our authors have boldly launched a shot at that moving target. We encourage you to engage, enjoy, and build upon their good work.

CLC
DMR
November 1995

Computers Can Read as Well as Count: How Computer-Aided Text Analysis Can Benefit Organisational Research

Boris Kabanoff

Queensland University of Technology, Australia

WHY CONTENT ANALYSIS?

The fact that computers can read as well as count is going to prove important for organisational behaviour (OB) researchers in the future. Let me begin my explanation of why I believe this by sharing with you the following observation. Over the years, as I have observed my non-OB, business school colleagues going about their research, one of the things that has struck me is that so many of them have such rich, large, and "naturally-generated" databases to work with. Accounting and finance researchers have access to vast amounts of data generated by organisations and stock exchanges; economists, of course, have the whole world generating various kinds of statistical data for them; while marketers have scanner data, TV ratings, sales figures, and so on to work with. Contrast this to the average OB researcher. In order to test his or her ideas the typical OB researcher usually runs a survey, conducts interviews, designs an experiment, and so on. Having to gather new data designed for answering some very specific issues probably has some advantages, but it also has a lot of disadvantages—time, cost, small samples, limited generalisability, lack of cumulation of research findings, scarcity of longitudinal data, reliance on intrusive forms of data gathering, and so on.

Trends in Organizational Behavior, Volume 3. Edited by C. L. Cooper and D. M. Rousseau
© 1996 John Wiley & Sons Ltd

So the question persisted: "Does OB have a natural, `self-generating' data source that can be used to investigate a wide range of behavioural issues in organisations?" When posed the question, the best most OB colleagues could come up with was "Well, I guess there are companies' personnel records". However, over the last few years, I have come to believe that OB does have such a natural source of data relevant for studying many types of OB questions—the text or documents that are generated by and about organisations as they go about their business. Text documents such as annual reports are produced regularly by organisations and over long periods of time. Text about organisations is also found in many other sources—newspapers, magazines, analysts' reports, and so on. Text analysis—or more broadly, content analysis—offers the means for using this data for research purposes.

CONTENT OR TEXT ANALYSIS (TA)

Stone, Dunphy, Smith and Ogilvie (1966, p. 5) defined content or text analysis (TA) as "any technique for making inferences by systematically and objectively identifying specified characteristics within text". Weber (1985), whose primer on content analysis must be considered essential reading by anyone interested in the subject, states that the core process of virtually all forms of TA is data reduction by which the many words of text are classified into much fewer content categories. While virtually all forms of TA rely to some extent on this "many words into few" approach, the extent to which the process of "word classification" is very explicitly specified and oriented to producing quantitative indices of textual content varies across different methods of TA. At the highly explicit, quantitative end is word-frequency-based TA, which is where computers can at present make their major contribution. Word-frequency-based analysis of text from various kinds of documents, and the contribution that computers can make to this process are our focus here. At the less explicit, non-quantitative end of the continuum are what have been termed more *cognitive mapping* approaches to TA. This usually involves more qualitative, "thematic" analysis of text and often relies upon interviews rather than upon documentary sources of text. Examples of various types of TA are found in the book *Mapping Strategic Thought* edited by Huff (1990); Weber (1985) concentrates on word-frequency-based analysis using computers, and a special issue of *Journal of Management Studies* (Eden, 1992), concentrates on the more qualitative end of the TA continuum.

Over the last few years, TA, both computer-aided and relying purely on human coders, has been used to study a number of important organisational issues, including:

- How managers explain good and poor organisational performance (Staw, McKechnie & Puffer, 1983).
- Whether managers conceal organisations' poor performance and which factors encourage or discourage them from doing this (Abrahamson & Park, 1994).
- How the managements of two railroad companies, one that survived and one that failed, interpreted changes in their environment and their strategic responses over a 25-year period (Barr, Stimpert & Huff, 1990).
- What the CEOs of surviving and non-surviving firms focused on during a business crisis (D'Aveni & MacMillan, 1990).
- How newspapers portrayed a high-profile business leader during his successes and subsequent decline (Chen & Meindl, 1991).
- The extent to which organisations express corporate social responsibility values in their annual reports (Wolfe, 1991).
- Whether organisations differ in the values they espouse and whether values have particular structures or patterns (Kabanoff, 1993).

Before we consider some of these studies in more detail, we briefly describe the basic TA process as a research methodology, its assumptions, and advantages.

TA: THE BASIC PROCESS

As already noted, virtually all forms of TA rely to some extent on classifying the words of text into a limited number of content or meaning categories. Therefore, development of a *coding scheme* is normally a central part of a TA study.

A coding scheme consists of a set of content categories. Each content category contains a number of words or phrases that are presumed to have a similar, shared meaning. For example, words that a company uses when referring to employee performance would include, among others, "performance", "achievement", "service", "efficiency", and so on. A coding scheme usually comprises a set of such content categories, the selection of these being based upon the issue being investigated and theory guiding the research. Frequently, especially in the context of computer-aided text analysis (CATA), a coding scheme will be called a *content analysis dictionary*.

Weber (1985, pp. 21–24) and Wolfe, Gephart and Johnson (1993) have provided detailed descriptions of the basic TA process; here we stress the following. The time that is spent on developing, refining, and testing the reliability and validity of a coding scheme is absolutely central to the confidence that can be placed on the conclusions based on TA research.

Just as a survey researcher needs well-constructed, reliable, valid survey questions, and an experimenter needs well-designed, well-executed experiments, the TA researcher needs to devote lots of time, attention, and creativity to the development of a coding scheme.

BASIC ASSUMPTIONS OF TA

Basic assumptions of TA have been well discussed by Huff (1990) and Woodrum (1984), as well as Weber (1985). Probably *the* core assumption of TA is that language plays a major role in how people perceive and understand their world; therefore, if we can analyse language, we gain insight into how people perceive and understand their world. That is, *words* are a *window* into important features of people's "world view". A frequently quoted example of this notion of "language as a reflection of mind" is the fact that Inuit people have names for, and presumably perceive, 20 different kinds of snow because of its importance in their lives. Word-frequency-based TA assumes that word frequency reflects the importance or *cognitive centrality* of a concept or construct either to the person who produced the text or to the intended audience for the text. The more frequently a word or theme occurs, the more central or important it is. There is some general evidence for the validity of the view. For example, Weber (1985, pp. 64–68) describes studies from at least three different countries that have identified the same pattern: the frequency with which political texts refer to issues related to wealth creation and to economic concerns is related to the state of the economy—economic decline is associated with an increased frequency of economic or wealth references while economic growth is associated with declining wealth concerns. While this finding in itself may not be very surprising, it has important implications for how we can study a wide range of other issues and concerns in text. As previously noted, content analysis assumes that *related* words can be grouped to identify overall themes of importance. That is, while words such as "performance" and "service" are different, they have a common, underlying concern—the level of people's task achievement. The frequency of word use can change over time, and is usually interpreted as an indication of a change in the level of attention and concern being given to an issue. The link between the frequency of words concerned with wealth-creation and economic conditions that we have just listed is an example of this connection.

Finally, juxtaposition of words can in some circumstances be interpreted as an indication of a mental connection between different themes or concerns. For example, Kabanoff, Waldersee and Cohen (1995) examined which kinds of themes were correlated with the discussion of organisational change in companies' annual reports. They concluded that organisations that espoused different kinds of values tended to portray change differently and in keeping with their espoused values. Another example is the coding system McClelland developed (McClelland, Atkinson, Clark & Lowell, 1953) for scoring stories for the presence of achievement imagery (see also McClelland, 1976). We won't describe the complete coding scheme, but give just two examples. McClelland reasoned that achievement imagery was present when a statement describing successful goal achievement was followed by a statement of positive affect (i.e., success + positive affect), such as the following: "The man wanted fame and got it—he died happy". Equally, however, achievement imagery can be involved when failure is followed by a statement of negative affect, such as: "The experiment failed and the scientist felt very disappointed" (i.e., failure + negative affect). By scoring many different kinds of text (such as primary school readers from different historical periods and countries) for the presence of such imagery McClelland and his colleagues have been able to investigate quantitatively the influence of variations in strength of achievement motive upon the behaviour of both individuals and entire societies. Scoring systems that involve scoring text for the presence of interrelated categories obviously require a higher level of theoretical understanding and are more difficult to develop. Such uses of TA show that word-frequency based analyses can be used to explore quite complex concepts and that word-frequency-based analysis, while seemingly simple and naïve can be quite sophisticated and able to provide valid indicators of important symbolic content in text.

THE ADVANTAGES OF TA RESEARCH

The benefits and advantages of TA research have been enumerated by a number of writers (e.g., Erdener & Dunn, 1990; Wolfe, Gephart & Johnson, 1993; Woodrum, 1984). I will concentrate here on those advantages that are likely to be most important to OB researchers.

Quality and Quantity

One of the benefits of TA is that it combines desirable characteristics from what are generally considered two separate, even inimical research traditions—qualitative and quantitative research. By allowing us to deal systematically with, and to quantify what are normally considered qualitative data such as documents and interviews, TA helps address the criticisms of sterility and lack of relevance that are sometimes directed at traditional, quantitative forms of research. At the same time, TA permits those of us who believe that, in the end, being able to quantify a phenomenon is desirable, to convert qualitative data to a quantitative form.

Natural and Unobtrusive

As pointed out at the very beginning of this chapter, TA can make available entirely new sources of data for OB researchers. At present the most frequently studied organisational texts are companies' annual reports (AR). Clearly, however, there are other kinds of texts that can be useful, such as newspaper reports (Fombrun & Shanley, 1990), internal magazines (Kabanoff, 1993), internal memos (Huff, 1983), and other kinds of special reports on specific organisational issues such as safety (Gephart, 1993). A feature of all these forms of text is that they are naturally produced, in the sense of not being produced for the researcher's purpose, and they can be unobtrusively accessed. This is not meant to imply that such texts necessarily provide valid or objective indicators of organisational processes or policies simply because they were produced by the organisation, but they do represent how an organisation naturally presents or projects itself to its normal audience, rather than to a researcher.

Longitudinal

The opportunity to carry out longitudinal research is clearly enhanced by the use of text analysis. For example Barr, Stimpert and Huff (1990) were able to trace the evolution of two railway companies' different strategies for dealing with a changing business environment by closely studying companies' ARs over a 25-year period. From this careful qualitative and quantitative analysis they felt they gained insight into what the surviving company had focused on and how it had responded to change, and how this differed from the management of the company that failed. The concept of attention pattern or attention focus (Cyert & March, 1992, pp. 40–41) is a central mechanism within Cyert and March's (1992) behavioural theory of the firm. Within the theory, an attention-focus mechanism is seen as playing a central role in how organisations select and develop their goals. We might say that, in effect, organisations are or become what they pay attention to. D'Aveni and MacMillan (1990) identified 57 large organisations that became bankrupt and paired them with 57 surviving firms that were similar in size and product/market environment. They then compared what the CEOs of failed and surviving firms had focused on during a business crisis. For example, they compared how often CEOs referred to internal versus external organisational concerns and issues, by coding the contents of CEOs' letters to shareholders and making statistical comparisons. What is immediately obvious about the use of TA in such studies is that it enabled researchers to study organisations over a period of time; to infer what the top managements of these different firms were focusing on in different periods, to make quantitative comparisons, and to sample strategically so as to identify organisations that confronted similar environments but had different outcomes.

Analysing organisational documents in order to gain insight into differences in organisational concerns and strategies is in our view often preferable to relying on retrospective accounts by managers of what they did in the past, or asking managers to say what they would do in response to a business scenario. A study by Golden (1992) indicates the potential limitations of retrospective reporting. Golden asked CEOs to report their firms' current strategies, and, two years later, he again asked them to report their firm's strategies of two years earlier. Of these retrospective accounts, 58% did not agree with the previous and validated reports of past strategy. TA can produce a less biased assessment of an organisation's strategic concerns than self-report.

Insight into Cognitive Processes

The use of organisational documents, such as annual reports, also gives us some degree of access to the concerns and thinking of the members of the organisation's top-team, to whom it is likely to be difficult to gain direct research access. Top management, even if it uses assistance from public relations specialists to "polish" an annual report, is usually concerned to shape the document in a way that reflects the intentions, concerns and "tactics" of the senior management group. The recent surge of interest in the characteristics of top-teams and how these relate to organisational strategies (e.g., see Sparrow's, 1994, review) has focused mainly upon the study of demographic characteristics of top-teams, largely because such data are fairly readily accessible. As Sparrow remarked however, the link between a top-team's demography and organisational strategies will not be fully convincing until we demonstrate the cognitive and social process linkages between these two sets of variables, and at present these linkages are merely inferred, or a "black box". Accessing the ongoing mental processes of members of top-teams will never be easy but TA has the potential to tell us something about the cognitive process of the top-team and thus illuminate the inner workings of that black-box.

Multi-methods

Text analysis also allows us to "triangulate" an issue by using different methods and sources of data, thus providing an opportunity for testing whether different approaches converge on the same answer. Thus we can measure organisational values by asking organisational members to describe the values of their organisations (e.g., Chatman & Jehn, 1994), but also study them by analysing the content of organisational documents, such as annual reports (e.g., Kabanoff, 1993). Individuals' reports about organisation's values may be coloured by their own values, their position in the organisation, tenure, and so on, whereas annual reports may contain values that senior managers would like to convince both internal and external audiences that an organisation has. Using two different methods to measure organisational values provides a good cross-check on the results from any one method (cf. Rokeach, 1979). A comparison of these two sets of value measures might even be a good way of assessing the extent to which an organisation has an organisation-wide value consensus or corporate culture (Trice & Beyer, 1993, p. 13).

The Other Advantages of CATA

By and large these are advantages that accrue to both manual and computer-aided text analysis. However CATA also has a number of unique advantages. *Perfect reliability*—classification of text by multiple human coders permits the level of reliability achieved to be assessed, while classification by computer leads to perfect reliability since the coding rules are applied in the same way by the software. Reliability is of course different from validity but it is nice to know that once you have developed a valid coding schema the computer will be your tireless, errorless clerk that does not get bored by the task of classifying large amounts of data over and over again.

Standard dictionaries—over time a number of "generic" content-analytic dictionaries have been developed which contain categories useful in many social science contexts. For example the Harvard Psycho-Social IV (Züll, Weber & Mohler, 1989) dictionary consists of some 80 categories developed to operationalise a "general theory of action" and, as its name suggests, the categories are based upon concepts from sociology and psychology. The development of such dictionaries can be considered the CATA equivalent of the development of standardised measurement tools in various areas of psychology, such as tests of personality, ability, intelligence, attitudes and so on. Rather than each researcher having to develop entirely new coding schemes from the ground up, the use of standard content categories from well-validated, general dictionaries is efficient and can enhance both the comparability and validity of TA studies. Unfortunately at present few such dictionaries have been developed and those that have been are not readily available.

Efficiency—a major drawback of manual methods of text analysis is their labour-intensive nature and inflexibility, which makes them highly unsuitable for exploratory work. Once a group of human coders have begun to code a body of text the process must continue, even if halfway through the researcher thinks of another important category or a better way of coding an existing category. On the other hand, a computer-based dictionary can be fairly readily refined as the researcher's knowledge about the text increases and reapplied to the same text, or to new text that is collected.

EXEMPLARS: WHAT TA CAN TELL US

Let us now examine in greater detail how a number of researchers have made use of TA and CATA to study several OB issues. After we have seen how a number of researchers have made good use of TA we will also provide some indications of its limitations; however, we will keep our discussion of TA's limitations until later. It will also be noted that we describe studies that used both manual and computer-aided forms of TA, this simply reflects the fact that studies relying on CATA are, at this stage, relatively rare.

Explaining Good and Bad Times

Staw, McKechnie and Puffer (1983) investigated whether management used self-serving attributions to justify the level of organisational performance. Self-serving attributions are causal attributions that allow people to take the blame for successes and avoid the blame for failures. For example, if you become interested in CATA as a result of reading this chapter, then clearly I am a persuasive writer, however if you show no increase in interest, you are clearly a narrow-minded person who is biased against new approaches! Self-serving attributions sure are handy!

Staw and his colleagues argued that if senior managers use self-serving attributions when justifying organisations' performance, then letters to shareholders in the annual reports of low-performing companies will tend to attribute the causes of organisational performance to external factors such as a downturn in industry demand or weakness in the general economy. High-performing corporations, on the other hand, should attribute their performance to internal causes like good products, good staff, and good planning by management.

The study focused on 49 high-performing and 32 low-performing companies, and analysed the kinds of explanations that were given for a company's performance in the annual letter to shareholders found in each company's annual report. The following is one example of the kind of causal explanation that was studied: "Questor Educational Products turned in disappointing results, partially due to the erratic purchasing pattern which emerged in the toy industry" (Staw, McKechnie & Puffer, 1983, p. 587). Such causal events were coded for locus of causality (internal or external to the company), positive or negative cause, and positive or negative effect.

Staw and his colleagues admitted that the coding process was not as simple as it might seem, and that ambiguities that can be excluded in an experiment or survey inevitably arise when we rely on analysing normal language. They commented (p. 588), "In fact, the most difficult aspect of coding... was specifying causal events themselves". For example, consider whether you would call the following sentence a causal explanation of organisational performance: "To achieve the high performance goals we had set ourselves at the beginning of the year meant we all had to work hard to overcome fierce competition from domestic and foreign competitors". Of course, looked at in another way this very fact is a good reason for analysing normal language in order to understand how people naturally explain causality. Even though we can reduce such "unfortunate ambiguities" by using a questionnaire that requires people to think about causality in ways specified by a researcher, we also lose a key part of the central phenomenon. Clearly there's room for both approaches but at present we know much less about how people explain causality in normal language than how they respond to attributional rating scales.

Despite ambiguities, the study achieved quite high levels of inter-rater reliability. That is, raters agreed overall about what kinds of attributions were being made in each letter to shareholders, even if they were focusing on different, specific causal explanations. In general, it is preferable to have evidence of reliable coding at the level of specific sentences rather than at the level of overall documents (Weber, 1985) because, as you can imagine, longer pieces of text can contain different, or even conflicting, themes and raters may focus on different parts of a longer piece of text and thereby give different codings.

The results from Staw, McKechnie and Puffer (1983) were quite interesting though not as straightforward as the researchers had hypothesised. Both successful and unsuccessful companies partly explained performance as due to negative external events; however unsuccessful companies made more frequent references to negative, external causes—they "doth protest too much", perhaps. A possible implication is that successful companies explain their performance in terms of their ability to overcome negative environmental effects while unsuccessful companies simply focus upon the negative events as a cause of poor outcomes. These explanatory processes were related to other important outcomes. The more that organisations, both high- and low-performing, emphasised positive events, that is enhanced their explanations, the more their share prices increased after the release of the annual report. That is, enhancement seemed to affect share price positively. However the more enhancement there was, the more stock that was sold by corporate executives in the months after the AR, suggesting that the enhancing statements were mainly impression management rather than positive expectations actually held by management. The Staw, McKechnie and Puffer (1983) study represented a clever use of natural data to test a psychological hypothesis about an important managerial activity and found that the process it studied seemed to have important consequences for organisations' outcomes in the "real world". A very satisfying result for any OB researcher.

What Factors Encourage Managers to Conceal Poor Outcomes

While Staw, McKechnie and Puffer studied 82 organisations, Abrahamson and Park (1994) studied over 1000 presidents' letters contained in ARs. The main issue they were interested in was related to that investigated by Staw, McKechnie and Puffer (1983)—the concealment of negative outcomes—but they focused more upon how the presence of outside directors, the amount of share ownership among external directors, and the size of institutional investors influenced concealment. To deal with the large amount of text involved. Abrahamson and Park (1994) used a combination of computer-aided and manual analysis.

They first used the computer to identify and count the frequency with which different words appeared in all 1000 plus ARs. Coders then identified all the words that had a potentially negative connotation for organisations and that appeared relatively frequently; some 60 words were identified, including such words as "adverse", "concern", "loss", "crash", "deteriorate", and so on. The computer was then asked to identify all of the paragraphs in presidents' letters that contained a negative word. Two coders then read each paragraph and decided whether the negative word was referring to a negative organisational outcome or not. For example, use of the word "disappointing" was coded as negative in the following sentence: "Some of the disappointing operating results in 1988 flowed from internal performance shortfalls in a number of areas", but the words "flat" and "negative" were not coded as negative in the following sentence: "Since these investments were made, restaurant sales have continued to climb in a year in which other restaurants have had flat or negative sales gains". Coders inserted coding symbols directly into computer files containing the texts of the presidents' letters, and these were then counted and summed for each letter by the computer. The study then examined which factors were associated with a high frequency of negative words.

A feature of the Abrahamson and Park (1994) study is that it included a large number of variables which could be related to the frequency of negative statements in letters. These included organisational performance measures, such as: return on assets; level of share ownership by directors and company officers; the proportion of outside directors on the board; the share ownership profile of the company; auditors' reports; and level of share sales by directors and company officers after the release of the annual report. Overall, the study supported the general findings by Staw, McKechnie and Puffer (1983) that there was a tendency to conceal negative outcomes but it went further in identifying the factors that influenced how much managers tended to conceal or reveal negative organisational outcomes. The factors that enhanced disclosure were negative changes in performances, a higher proportion of outside directors; the presence of large, institutional investors, and auditors' reports. Low disclosure was associated with the presence of small organisational investors and outside directors who were shareholders. This is an impressive replication and extension of the earlier work on managerial explanations of company performance given the size and diversity of the sample studied.

The study by Abrahamson and Park (1994) is a good demonstration of how computer-aided text analysis can allow researchers to deal in a systematic way with very large amounts of text without "burning out" human coders, and how text can be interpreted in relation to other measures of organisational structure and performance. It is also difficult to imagine how an alternative approach such as a survey could ever hope to test these types of hypotheses. Imagine asking CEOs to answer questions about concealment of negative outcomes by their organisations. Even if CEOs were inclined to answer truthfully they may not be fully conscious that they try to slant their explanations of a company's performance in particular ways, and one would also expect a high degree of post hoc rationalisation of such behaviour. Text analysis may be the only feasible way of accessing some cognitive processes into which people do not have a great deal of personal insight, or that they may be tempted to conceal, or to rationalise.

Abrahamson and Park's (1994) study represents a relatively simple and straightforward use of CATA in combination with manual coding. CATA was used mainly to identify the words to be coded, and to isolate portions of text that contained the words of interest—human coders then made the judgement about whether a negative word was being used in relation to organisational outcomes. In some respects the coding schema is quite primitive in comparison to, say, the schema developed by McClelland. Clearly, there are a number of other key questions that we could ask about how presidents' letters deal with negative organisational performance which go beyond asking simply how much "negativity" is present in letters. For example, do letters that articulate an organisational strategy for dealing with negative circumstances and for improving organisational performance result in improved future performance? To take a cue from D'Aveni and MacMillan's (1990) study mentioned earlier, what kinds of strategic concerns in presidents' letters lead to improved future performance? Is a focus on internal, organisational processes or on external, environmental processes more likely to result in an improvement? Measuring the presence of different kinds of strategic concerns is clearly a more complex and difficult task using CATA, but it is also a task that reduces the feasibility of relying on human coders. Consider the time and cost of asking coders to read and code 1000 presidents' letters for the presence and type of strategy being described. In cases such as this CATA simultaneously becomes both more difficult and more necessary.

The final study is considered in slightly greater detail because it relied to a far greater extent on CATA than either of the previous ones.

The Values Organisations Espouse

Kabanoff (1993), and Kabanoff, Waldersee and Cohen (1995) sought to measure differences in the kinds of values that organisations espouse in their annual reports, mission statements, and internal magazines. Specifically, based on earlier theoretical work (Kabanoff, 1991), they sought to show that organisations' values could be described in terms of four main types of value structures or value profiles. Kabanoff (1991, 1993) outlined how organisations seek to combine or balance between two major types of values: equity-oriented values that emphasise maximising organisational efficiency and economic outcomes, and equality-oriented values that emphasise interpersonal cohesion and solidarity among organisational members. He described four main ways in which organisations "combined" equity and equality (or efficiency and cohesion) concerns with each of these four ways representing a distinctive value structure and type of organisation. A value structure can be defined as an overall value pattern in which values can be combined in both complementary and conflicting ways—some structures emphasise only complementary values while others emphasise values that involve some degree of conflict between the espoused values. The four types were:

(1) *Elite*: emphasises only equity values (performance, reward, authority) while de-emphasising equality or cohesion values (affiliation, participation, normative, teamwork, commitment, leadership).
(2) *Leadership*: a variation of the Elite type which, while emphasising equity values, also emphasises some cohesion values (leadership, teamwork, commitment, affiliation), but not participation and normative values.
(3) *Collegial*: the most equality-oriented type which emphasises equality values (participation, affiliation, normative, teamwork, commitment), but not equity values or leadership.
(4) *Meritocratic*: a variation of the Collegial type which emphasises the equality values of the Collegial type, but also emphasises some equity values, namely reward and performance.

In principle, it would be possible to gather information about organisations' values by asking organisational members to describe what they perceived to be the organisation's values; however, there are both practical and theoretical obstacles to doing this. The practical difficulties need little explanation. Since we are interested in describing the values of organisations, organisations are the unit of analysis and there are considerable difficulties involved in obtaining representative samples of respondents from a reasonable number of organisations. Also in theory terms, an unobtrusive approach that did not require organisational members to act as reporters on organisational values seemed preferable since we believed we were studying underlying, almost unconscious value patterns that individual members may not be directly aware of. Therefore an approach that allowed us to search for these patterns in organisations' natural expressions of their concerns and values seemed appropriate. Text analysis offered an unobtrusive means for measuring organisations' espoused values and also gave us the potential to measure espoused values over a period of time, which should provide a more reliable indication of organisational values than a study at a single point in time. As Rokeach (1979, p. 53) observed, *organisations can be expected to leave traces of their distinctive value patterns in their documents*.

Documents from 88 large Australian organisations, including annual reports, internal magazines and mission statements, were collected and sections of these documents which dealt with or were likely to deal with organisational values, such as the CEO's annual letter to shareholders, were extracted for analysis.

A content-analysis dictionary based upon the values specified by the theory was developed. This included the nine core values shown in Table 1.1.

More than a million words of text were read by computer programs which searched for references to those nine values. The relative "density" with which different values were referred to in company documents was estimated by dividing the number of times each value was referred to by the total number of sentences from each company that was analysed. Thus each company received nine value scores based upon the relative frequency with which each of the nine values was referred to in its documents. While it would be possible simply to compare or profile organisations in terms of their scores on different values, our aim was to discover whether organisations' value profiles could be characterised in terms of a limited number of different value

Table 1.1 The computer-based content analysis dictionary

Category	Definition and examples
Authority	Concern with authority figures and relations, e.g., executive, manager, director
Leadership	Concern with leadership, e.g., leader, leadership
Team	Concerned with teams and teamwork, e.g., team, teamwork, cooperation
Participation	Concerned with participation by non-managerial levels, e.g., participation, consultation co-occurs with reference to employees
Commitment	Concerned with organisational commitment and loyalty, e.g., commitment, loyalty, dedication
Performance	Concerned with performance, e.g., achievement, performance, service, efficiency
Reward	Concerned with organisational reward system, especially remuneration, e.g., bonus, compensation, reward, salary
Affiliation[a]	All words with connotation of affiliation or supportiveness, e.g., share, enthusiasm, appreciate, join together
Normative[a] (Rectitude	All rectitude values invoking in the final analysis the social order and its demands as the justification, e.g., responsibilities, ethics) fair, rights

[a]Affiliation comes from the Harvard IV dictionary and Normative is the Rectitude (Ethics) category from the Lasswell dictionary. Both dictionaries come from *The General Inquirer III* (Züll, Weber & Mohler, 1989).

patterns specified by theory. That is, were there organisations that resembled each one of the four, theoretical types—the Elite, Leadership, Collegial and Meritocratic?

A form of theory-based cluster analysis was used to identify organisations that had value profiles that resembled the value profiles we would expect to find based upon the theory. Figure 1.1 shows the average value profiles of four groups of organisations that were selected on the basis of the resemblance of their actual value profile to one of our theoretical value profiles.

It can be seen in Figure 1.1 that the four clusters of organisations have fairly distinctive value profiles that approximate the theoretical value profiles. We would not expect to find that organisations matched the theoretical types exactly since the types are seen as representing theoretical ideals that need not exist in this form in the "real world" (see Doty & Glick's, 1994, recent discussion of this issue). Nevertheless, there was a Collegial group that put strong emphases on affiliation, participation and normative values, and a low emphasis on rewards. Universities and government departments tended to cluster in this group. There was also a Leadership group that put strong emphases on leadership, teamwork and loyalty values, and a Meritocratic group that had the expected combination of cohesion and performance values. The

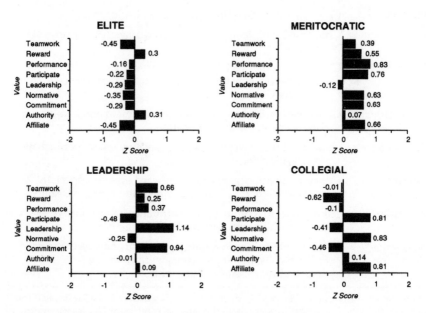

Figure 1.1   Value profiles of four types of value structures

profile for the Elite group was less pronounced. On the whole the results were interesting and fairly supportive of the theory. This study suggests that CATA can be used for comparing organisations in terms of espoused values. What future research needs to demonstrate is that these differences in espoused values relate in meaningful ways to differences in organisations' actual practices and policies.

CATA: THE PROMISE

For those of us who already are converts to this method of doing organisational research, CATA has a sense of excitement and potential about it that is, in the opinion of the author, unfortunately missing from most areas of OB at present. The excitement flows in large part from CATA's capacity to integrate a number of diverse and even opposing elements in OB, such as how to:

- do both qualitatively rich and quantitatively rigorous research
- observe and measure but not intrude during the process of doing so
- conduct longitudinal research but publish frequently
- have reasonable sample sizes but minimise costs of data gathering
- study cognitive processes of organisational members and relate these to organisational processes and also to the external environment

CATA has the potential to deal with these apparently conflicting demands, as has been demonstrated by a number of the studies we have discussed.

CATA: THE CURRENT STATE OF PLAY

A criticism of computer-aided methods when compared to manual analysis has been that they have lower context-sensitivity. That is, human coders are "smarter readers" and better able to judge the specific meaning that a word has within a particular context. For example, does the word "leader" in a sentence refer to a person or role in an organisation, or to the organisation being a "market leader" in a product category? This is the key issue of validity and it is an aspect that critics of CATA tend to focus on. Nevertheless we noted earlier in our discussion of McClelland's system that CATA can be more sophisticated than counting the frequency of a single word. Also, even when we accept that computers are not as smart as human readers, some research indicates that this apparent advantage of manual coding is less clear than people tend to suppose. Rosenberg, Schnurr and Oxman (1990) found that computer-aided text analysis using categories from the Harvard IV Psycho-Social dictionary outperformed human coders even in what we might expect to be a highly "context-sensitive" task—using samples of free speech to assign psychiatric patients from four different diagnostic groups to a diagnostic category. Rosenberg, Schnurr and Oxman (1990, p. 307) concluded: "the most parsimonious explanation [for the superiority of computer-based methods] appears to be that the reliability of computerised systems gives them an advantage in classifying texts, even if their classification schemata are based on the sheer number of utterance types in a text. ... it may be that the reliability of the system becomes an overriding factor if quantification is desired". That is not to say there aren't significant challenges to overcome.

A symposium on CATA at the 1994 Academy of Management National Conference demonstrated several areas in which CATA shows signs of its youthfulness as a methodology. Presenters in the symposium all relied on different text-analysis packages, and therefore were expending large amounts of time and effort on understanding the peculiarities of their own software system. At present, there appear to be no text-analysis packages that meet the requirements and standards of different researchers. Different researchers also tend to use somewhat different approaches for establishing the reliability and validity of their coding schema. Unlike the fairly well-established procedures for conducting survey, laboratory, or even case-based research, the rules for CATA are less well defined and certainly not taught in any research methods courses of which I am aware. This also means that journal reviewers, confronted by a CATA-based study, find themselves in an unusual and difficult situation. Without a clear set of criteria by which to judge this type of research, reviewers tend to fall back upon criteria that aren't always well suited to assessing CATA-type research. The underlying and normally desirable conservatism that is a feature of the reviewing process of most top-quality journals makes publishing CATA type research even more uncertain than is the case with research that uses more traditional methods.

HOW TO FIND OUT MORE ABOUT CATA

Two of the best applications of TA and CATA methodologies that I am aware of are to be found in the following two books: Namenwirth and Weber (1987), who use CATA to trace patterns of societal concerns over long periods, and McClelland (1976), who uses both TA and CATA to investigate the influence of the Need for Achievement motive at individual and societal levels. Kerlinger is one who was impressed by what McClelland had done, saying of it: "I know of no more ambitious and competent studies of a complex phenomenon and the testing of plausible hypotheses" (1986, p. 301). While neither book focuses on specifically OB issues, they represent good demonstrations of how to conduct ambitious, high-quality CATA-based research. The journal *Quality and Quantity* publishes text-analytic studies.

Three well known text-analysis packages are Textpack 4 (Mohler & Züll, 1990), The Minnesota Contextual Content Analysis package (McTavish & Pirro, 1990), and the General Inquirer III (Züll, Weber & Mohler, 1989). The latter package contains some of the best validated, general purpose dictionaries, but unfortunately runs in an IBM-mainframe environment. The most powerful and flexible program that can be used for general text retrieval that I am aware of is ISYS (ISYS, 1990). Text retrieval is closely related to text analysis (see Wolfe, Gephart & Johnson (1993)), but generally focuses more on the search and retrieval processes rather than on the actual analysis of semantic content. ISYS is very fast, handles huge amounts of text, runs in a Windows environment, and is excellent for building and refining coding categories. It is also able to work with more complex coding schemes involving the co-occurrence of multiple categories, and to handle coding categories including many different words. An inconvenient feature is that while it produces overall frequency counts on the screen, it does not provide frequency counts on a sentence-by-sentence basis, or generate an output file of frequencies on the computer which can then be subjected directly to further statistical analyses.

CONCLUSION

Dunphy, Bullard and Crossing (1989) observed: "Man's most distinctive characteristic as a species is his language-making ability and language behavior is the social scientists' major source of evidence about almost any social phenomenon in which he is interested. ... Yet much of the brief history of the development of quantitative methods in the social sciences reads like a search for ways of avoiding dealing with natural language. For years, social scientists concentrated on devising survey instruments which would force subjects into limited language responses. .." (p. 140). Perhaps this was inevitable when we believed that the main way in which computers could assist us in our research was their ability to process large amounts of numerical data. While this assumption was never strictly true it is now clear that the assumption is wholly out of place—computers can read as well as count. With this realisation can come a new and exciting period for what we study and how we study it in the field of organisational behaviour.

ACKNOWLEDGEMENTS

Thanks to Paul Nesbit, Robert Waldersee and Robert Wood for helpful comments.

REFERENCES

Abrahamson, E. & Park, C. (1994) Concealment of negative organisational outcomes: An agency theory perspective. *Academy of Management Journal*, **37**(5), 1–35.

Barr, P. S., Stimpert, J. L. & Huff, A. S. (1990) Cognitive change, strategic action, and organisational renewal. *Strategic Management Journal*, **13**(S), 15–36.

Bowman, E. H. (1984) Content analysis of annual reports for corporate strategy and risk. *Interfaces*, **14**(1), 61–71.

Chatman, J. A. & Jehn, K. A. (1994) Assessing the relationship between industry characteristics and organisational culture: How different can you be? *Academy of Management Journal*, **37**(3), 522–553.

Chen, C. & Meindl, J. R. (1991) The construction of leadership images in the popular press: The case of Donald Burr and the *People Express*. *Administrative Science Quarterly*, **36**, 521–551.

Cyert, R. M. & March, J. G. (1992) A behavioural theory of the firm. (2nd edn), Cambridge, MA: Blackwell.

D'Aveni, R. A. & MacMillan, I. (1990) Crisis and the content of managerial communication: A study of the focus of attention of top managers in surviving and failing firms. *Administrative Science Quarterly*, **36**, 634–657.

Doty, D. H. & Glick, W. H. (1994) Typologies as a unique form of theory building: Toward improved understanding and modelling. *Academy of Management Review*, **19**(2), 230–251.

Dunphy, D. C., Bullard, C. G. & Crossing, E. M. (1989) Validation of the General Inquirer Harvard IV Dictionary. In C. Züll, P. W. Weber & P. P. Mohler, *Computer-Aided Text Classification for the Social Sciences: The General Inquirer III*. Mannheim, Germany: ZUMA, The Centre for Surveys, Research and Methodology.

Eden, C. (1992) On the nature of cognitive maps. *Journal of Management Studies*, **29**(3), 261–265.

Erdener, C. & Dunn, C. P. (1990) Content analysis. In A. S. Huff (Ed.), *Mapping Strategic Thought*. Chichester, UK: Wiley.

Fombrun, C. & Shanley, M. (1990) What's in a name? Reputation building and corporate strategy. *Academy of Management Journal*, **33**, 233–258.

Gephart, R. P. (1993) The textual approach: Risk and blame in disaster sense making. *Academy of Management Journal*, **36**, 1464–1514.

Golden, B. R. (1992) The past is the past—or is it? The use of retrospective accounts as indicators of past strategy. *Academy of Management Journal*, **35**(4), 848–860.

Huff, A. S. (1983) A rhetorical examination of strategic change. In L. R. Pondy, P. J. Frost, G. Morgan & D. C. Dandridge (Eds), *Organisational Symbolism*. Greenwich, CT: JAI Press.

Huff, A. S. (1990) *Mapping Strategic Thought*. Chichester, UK: Wiley.

ISYS (1990) Text retrieval software for IBM and compatible personal computers and networks. Odyssey Development P/L, Crows Nest, Sydney, Australia.

Kabanoff, B. (1991) Equity, equality, power and conflict. *Academy of Management Review*, **16**, 416–441.

Kabanoff, B. (1993). An exploration of espoused culture in Australian organizations (with a closer look at the baulking sector). *Asia Pacific Journal of Human Resources*, **31**(3), 1–29.

Kabanoff, B. & Holt, J. (1994) Changes in the espoused values of Austrlian organisations 1986–1990. Paper presented at the National Academy of Management Conference, Dallas, Texas.

Kabanoff, B., Waldersee, R. & Cohen, M. (1995) Espoused organizational values and their relation to organizational change themes: A content-analytic study. *Academy of Management Journal*, **38**, 1075–1104.

Kerlinger, F. N. (1986) *Foundations of Behavioral Research* (3rd edn). New York: Holt, Rinehart & Winston.

McClelland, D. C. (1976) *The Achieving Society*. New York: Irvington.

McClelland, D. C., Atkinson, J. W., Clark, R. A. & Lowell, E. L. (1953) *The Achievement Motive*. New York: Appleton-Century-Crofts.

McTavish, D. G. & Pirro, E. B. (1990) Contextual content analysis. *Quality and Quantity*, **24**, 245–265.

Mohler, P. P. & Züll, C. (1990) Textpack P.C.Mannheim, Germany: ZUMA, The Centre for Surveys, Research and Methodology.

Namenwirth, J. Z. & Weber, R. P. (1987) *Dynamics of Culture*. Winchester, MA: Allen & Unwin.

Rokeach, M. (1979) From individual to institutional values: With special reference to the values of science. In M. Rokeach (Ed.) *Understanding Human Values*. New York: Free Press.

Rosenberg, S. D., Schnurr, P. P. & Oxman, T. E. (1990) Content analysis: a comparison of manual and computerised systems. *Journal of Personality Assessment*, **54**, 298–310.

Sparrow, P. R. (1994) The psychology of strategic management: Emerging themes of diversity and cognition. In C. L. Cooper & I. T. Robertson (Eds), *International Review of Industrial and Organizational Psychology*. Chichester, UK: Wiley.

Staw, B. M., McKechnie, P. I. & Puffer, S. M. (1983) The justification of organisational performance. *Administrative Science Quarterly*, **28**, 582–600.

Stone, P. J., Dunphy, D. C., Smith, M. S. & Ogilvie, D. M. (1966) *The General Inquirer: a Computer Approach to Content Analysis*. Cambridge, MA: M.I.T. Press.

Trice, H. M. & Beyer, J. M. (1993) *The Cultures of Work Organisations*. Englewood Cliffs, NJ: Prentice-Hall.

Weber, R. P. (1985) *Basic Content Analysis*. Beverly Hills, CA: Sage.

Wolfe, R. A. (1991) The use of content analysis to assess corporate responsibility. *Research in Corporate Social Performance and Policy*, **12**, 281–307.

Wolfe, R. A., Gephart, R. P. & Johnson, T. E. (199) Computer-facilitated data analysis: Potential contributions to management research. *Journal of Management*, **19**(3), 637–660.

Woodrum, E. (1984) Mainstreaming content analysis in social science: Methodological advantages, obstacles and solutions. *Social Science Research*, **13**, 1–19.

Züll, C., Weber, P. W. & Mohler, P. P. (1989) *Computer-aided Text Classification for the Social Sciences: The General Inquirer III*. Mannheim, Germany: ZUMA, The Centre for Surveys, Research and Methodology.

CHAPTER 2

Issues in Managerial Compensation Research

Matthew C. Bloom and George T. Milkovich

ILR School/Cornell University, Ithaca, New York, USA

> The ideas of economists and political philosophers, both when they
> are right and when they are wrong, are more powerful than is
> commonly understood. Indeed the world is ruled by little else.
> Practical (people) who believe themselves to be quite exempt from
> any intellectual influences are usually slaves of some defunct
> economist. Madmen in authority, who hear voices in the air, are
> distilling their frenzy from some academic scribbler of a few years
> back. I am sure the power of vested interests is vastly exaggerated
> compared with the gradual encroachment of ideas. (John Maynard
> Keynes, from R. L. Heilbroner, *The Worldly Philosophers*)[1]

Compensation is at the core of any employment exchange (Milkovich &
Newman, 1993; Simon, 1951). It is probably the most basic reason people
agree to become employees and it serves as a defining characteristic of
any employment relationship (March & Simon, 1958). Recently, managers
have been bombarded with a profusion of ways to pay employees. There
is team-based pay, broad-banding, pay at risk, paying for competencies,
paying for skills, and even "The New" pay. Understanding which of
these have the potential to add value and which are relatively more
effective is a tough task, like untying the Gordian knot. Rather than
simply cutting through the problem (Alexander the Great's tack),
managers often seek guidance from research. Yet, researchers have also
been bombarded—not just with new practices, but also with new
theories. Included in this theoretical barrage are agency theory,

---

[1] We note that Lord Keynes' remarks apply equally well to psychologists, sociologists, and
statisticians whose ideas find their way into use and misuse by practical people.

Trends in Organizational Behavior, Volume 3. Edited by C. L. Cooper and D. M. Rousseau
© 1996 John Wiley & Sons Ltd

tournament models, contingency theory, institutional theory, procedural justice, political influence theory, organizational demography, resource dependency, psychological contracts, and the resource-based view of the firm. The list seems almost endless. If Lord Keynes is correct that theories drive practical people's decisions, understanding which of these theories are useful and which are not is important both for compensation researchers and for practical decision makers.

Traditionally, theories about compensation have been classified according to the questions they address (Gomez-Mejia & Balkin, 1992; Mahoney, 1979). Some treat managerial pay and pay systems as outcomes (i.e., the dependent variable), offering answers to questions about what factors explain differences in managerial pay (Figure 2.1). Others treat pay and pay systems as causes (i.e., the independent variable), answering questions about how compensation decisions will affect managers' attitudes and behavior and, ultimately, organizational performance.

While such classifications are useful, they may also mislead. To better understand the potential consequences of any pay system requires that we *simultaneously* account for the features of the pay system itself (treating pay as an independent variable) and related contextual features that may influence the consequences and outcomes of the pay system (treating pay as a dependent variable) (see Figure 2.2). *The point is that*

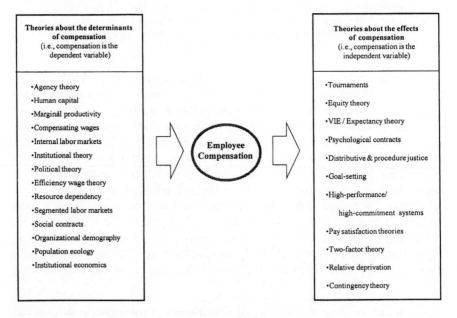

Figure 2.1 Classification of compensation theories

context matters. The impact of any managerial pay plan is influenced by the *environment* in which it operates (e.g., tax codes, economic conditions, public policy), the *organization* adopting the plan (e.g., ownership structure, level of firm risk, organization site), and the *individual* managers covered by the plan (e.g., risk-taking attitudes, human capital factors, personal needs and goals). These contextual factors are the essence of theories which treat pay as an outcome. For example, human capital theory suggests managerial attributes which affect individual earnings (e.g., experience, education, skills); resource dependence and internal labor market theories offer guidance about factors in the organization and work itself which affect managerial pay (e.g., control over critical resources, hierarchy, required skills); and agency theory introduces factors such as risk aversion and information availability which drive the compensation preferences of managers and organizations.

When we consider the range of theoretical views which have been applied to compensation, we question how much leverage each provides us in terms of understanding both context and consequences and whether there are any fundamental principles linking them. Twenty-five years ago Mahoney (1979, p. 4) pointed out that:

> [n]o comprehensive theory of employee compensation exists at present. Rather, there exists a number of segmented theories or models of compensation and employee behavior as well as numerous empirical observations focusing on specific aspects of compensation and employee

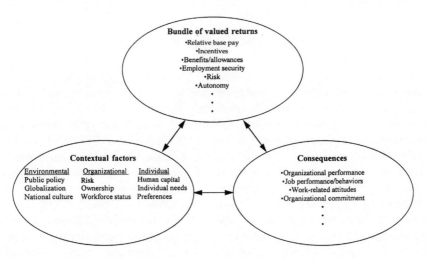

Figure 2.2 The bundle of valued returns, context, and consequences

behavior. These segmented approaches to analysis and understanding of compensation issues largely reflect the fact that each is directed toward answering a relatively specific question, a question different from questions addressed by other approaches.

The only difference between then and now is that more "segmented approaches"—additional theories—have been added to the list. Lord Keynes leaves little doubt that theories can be important guides for decision makers and scholars. Theories specify what is important and why, how things are related, and the conditions which affect these relationships (Campbell, 1990). Mahoney (1979, p. ix) concurs, "I believe that a good theory will outlive any specific application of that theory in practice. Practice will change with varying circumstances, yet good theory is independent of those circumstances and ought to guide changes in practice". Theory ought to be able to explain what works and what does not, for sure. But if theory is to be useful, it must also help us solve problems, meet changing conditions, anticipate the impact of important trends, and inform us about the impact of changes in compensation systems and policies. Therein lies the need to include both context and consequences when we examine managerial compensation. In this chapter we highlight some of the important issues we believe compensation theory and research should address. Our list is not exhaustive, but it does capture some of the most important problems, changing conditions, and challenges that are shaping the compensation decisions managers will be facing. We begin by reconsidering the definition of compensation.

REDEFINING COMPENSATION

Adam Smith was among the first to propose a formal theory of the relationship between compensation and work. He characterized pay in terms of the "net advantage" resulting from an exchange of multiple returns which, when added and subtracted, determine what the worker will provide to the employer (Mahoney, 1979; Smith, 1776/1976). Smith's original formalization notwithstanding, researchers have largely treated compensation as unidimensional. Fostered by psychological and economic views which emphasized the exchange of pay for effort (Ehrenberg & Smith, 1991; Opsahl & Dunnette, 1966; Lawler, 1971), compensation has for many years been narrowly defined as the pecuniary returns an organization offers its employees. Recently, a few emerging theories are returning to a broader view, defining compensation as a *bundle of valued returns* offered in exchange for a *cluster of employee contributions* (Bloom, 1996; Cappelli & Rogovsky, 1994; Gerhart & Milkovich, 1993; Tsui, Pearce, Porter & Hite, 1995). Under this "bundle of valued returns" view, the set of returns an organization offers is an interrelated collection—a set of reparations, benefits, and items of value. Both practice and theory inform us about possible elements of this bundle. Certainly cash pay is one. Benefits such as health care, disability, and life insurance, vacations, sick leave, sabbatics, and perquisites such as country club memberships, car allowances, and expense accounts are others (Miceli & Lane, 1991). Theories suggest elements such as employment security (Osterman, 1988), mutual support (Eisenberger, Faslo & Davis-LaMastro, 1990), trust (Smith, 1992), opportunities for self-actualization (Schein, 1980), working toward mutually valued goals, and even the joys of being part of an ongoing commitment which one values (James & James, 1992) are too. Rather than viewing the employment relationship as a series of bivariate associations (e.g. pay for work), the bundle of valued returns view shifts our attention from an exclusive focus on cash-based pay to the relationship among all valued returns. Implicit in this view is Adam Smith's premise about net advantage; that the outcomes of almost any compensation decision are influenced to a greater or lesser extent by other valued returns included in the bundle. For example, the effects of incentive pay on managerial behaviors probably depend upon the level of employment security, autonomy to affect results, and the degree of trust underlying the employment exchange (Baker, Jensen & Murphy, 1988; Bloom & Milkovich, 1995; Huselid, 1995). Certain bundles may elicit one set of employee responses quite different from the outcomes of another bundle. Beyond beliefs and anecdotes, very little is known about the profile of these bundles, the potential trade-offs among valued returns, and what they mean for both the organization and the manager. Barringer and Milkovich (1995) report that managers are highly sensitive to changes in the mix of elements comprising total compensation. Reductions in employment security and earnings appear to be associated with lower job and pay satisfaction and increased interest in finding a new job. Excluding this study there is virtually no empirical work examining compensation as a bundle of valued returns.

Two theories may offer some guidance here: psychological contracts theory (Macneil, 1980, 1985; Rousseau & Parks, 1993) and resource-based theory (Barney, 1990; Wright, McMahan & McWilliams, 1994). Psychological contracts theory views the relationship between employer and employee as a collection of promises; a set of obligations to exchange contributions for returns. As this exchange becomes less like a simple sales transaction and more like an ongoing relationship, the location of valued returns moves from an exclusive focus on cash wages to a variety of socio-emotional benefits (Macneil, 1980, 1985; Rousseau & Parks, 1993). Psychological contracts theory asserts that what the organization offers (i.e., the bundle of valued returns) is crucial for understanding what the employee contributes in exchange. Psychological contracts are schemas (Cantor, 1990) which give meaning to the bundle and direct individual reactions to it. Simple monetary returns evoke basic effort to meet current work conditions. Mutuality and commitment on behalf of the organization elicit reciprocal commitment and also, perhaps, creativity and innovation from the manager (Eisenberger, Huntington, Hutchison & Sowa, 1986; Eisenberger, Faslo & Davis-LaMastro, 1990). Consequently, psychological contracts theory might offer some leverage for understanding the effects of various bundles of valued returns (see Rousseau & Parks, 1993, and the special issue of *Human Resource Management*, 1994, *33*, no. 2). Investigating how differences in these bundles affect managers' psychological contracts may be one approach to this issue.

Resource-based theory (RBT) shifts the focus to the organizational level of analysis. It predicts that sustaining a competitive advantage derives from gaining preferential access to and maximizing unique resources, including human resources (Barney, 1990; Wright, Smart & McMahan, in press). The organization determines what unique human resource capabilities (e.g., innovativeness, sophisticated technical knowledge) it possesses and chooses a particular bundle of valued returns to optimize their use (Cappelli & Singh, 1992; Wright et al, 1994). RBT is a twist on the strategic-contingent model which asserts compensation must be tailored to "fit" the business strategy and environment of the organization (Gomez-Mejia & Balkin, 1992; Milkovich & Newman, 1993). Under RBT, an organization's HR capabilities may determine its business strategy. Hence, the bundle of valued returns must be tailored to "fit" these HR capabilities, simultaneously attracting, retaining, eliciting, and directing them toward organizational goals. If innovativeness is a unique capability, the bundle should elicit its use to achieve and sustain the organization's competitive advantage. One research direction provoked by RBT is to study how changes in the bundle affect the exhibition and use of HR capabilities and what bundles do indeed support a sustained competitive advantage.

Research into the bundle of valued returns is just beginning and even the most basic questions remain to be answered:

- What should be included and excluded from the bundle? What are the critical elements and interrelationships?
- What factors (environmental, organizational, individual) determine the nature of this bundle?

- How does the bundle of valued returns exert its influence on managerial attitudes and behaviors? Do differences in the bundle an organization offers affect managerial attitudes and performance (Barringer & Milkovich, 1995)?

In sum, the bundle of valued returns changes our definition of compensation. It suggests that the interactions among the components of the employment contract are critical (and largely unstudied) determinants of employee attitudes and behaviors and organizational performance. As Figure 2.2 suggests, the critical challenge is determining if such a broad view adds to our understanding of workplace behaviors and performance. Or, does it simply muddy the waters? Once the bundle of valued returns is defined—what should be included and excluded, what are the key interrelationships—research can address the likely outcomes of these bundles and the contextual factors which affect both the relationships and their outcomes.

THE IMPORTANCE OF CONTEXT

We have already noted that context permeates issues about why compensation systems are structured as they are and what they are likely to end up producing. In so doing we join others who have called for scholars to take up issues related to context in organizational research (Gerhart & Milkovich, 1993; Jackson & Schuler, 1995; James, Demaree, Mulaik & Ladd, 1992). In this section we explore some of these contextual factors and consider how they might influence both the components of the bundle of valued returns and its related outcomes.

The Missing Role of Risk

Theory and practice tell us that risk—uncertainty about future events—is critical for understanding compensation (Eisenhardt, 1989; Levinthal, 1988). The popular business literature warns that constantly changing competitive environments impose uncertainty on organizations and employees (Drucker, 1992; Hammer & Champy, 1993). Organizational strategy researchers have demonstrated that risk influences business strategies, organizational performance, and the decisions managers make (Bromiley & Curley, 1992; Hill, Hitt & Hoskisson, 1992; Miller & Bromiley, 1990). Yet, little is known about the relationships among risk, compensation, managerial behaviors, and organizational performance.

Two recent studies indicate that risk does have important effects on compensation decisions and outcomes. Using data from initial public offerings, Beatty and Zajac (1994) find organizational risk is negatively associated with the use of performance-based pay (e.g., stock options). A study by Bloom and Milkovich (1995) also indicates that business risk is negatively related to the use of performance-based compensation, this time in a sample of 360 large, established companies. Their evidence further suggests that business risk mitigates the effects of incentive pay plans on organizational performance; businesses operating in high-risk situations which also rely more heavily on incentive pay exhibit poorer performance. Apparently risk does matter, at least for understanding performance-based pay.

Risk might also be responsible for the persistent problem of motivating managers to take future-oriented actions. Compensating managers so they will make decisions with the long-run interests of the organization in mind is difficult since these decisions often impose greater risk on managers' income (Hoskisson, Hitt, Turk & Tyler, 1989; Walsh & Seward, 1990). Too much risk might induce managers to spend time trying to reduce it rather than focusing on critical organizational goals (Amit & Wernerfelt, 1990). Or, it might have the opposite effect—inducing managers to become reckless in their risk taking. Context again seems to play a part. Managers seem to be more risk taking when faced with losses and risk averse when faced with gains (Kahneman, Slovic & Tversky, 1982). Kanfer (1990) suggests some form of volitional, self-regulating process underlies the goal–pay–performance relationships. Following her logic, uncertainty in organizations will mediate the effects of performance-based pay on managers' behaviors. Indeed, there may be an optimal level of compensation risk—variability in pay up to a point is motivating, but beyond that point it becomes dysfunctional. This optimal level of risk may be discretionary given the components of the bundle of valued returns.

So far we have discussed risk as a component of context. Risk might also be an element of the bundle of valued returns. Internal labor markets theory stresses the importance of stable employment and the potential trade-offs higher security might provide (Kochan & Osterman, 1994; Pfeffer, 1994; Osterman, 1988). Here, increased security (less risk) is a return offered to managers. On the other hand, some people seem to like risky situations, viewing them as opportunities to be exploited (Lopes, 1987; Schneider & Lopes, 1986). This might explain why some managers choose commission-based jobs and others prefer jobs with base pay alone. Although compensation theories offer limited direction, we need to begin addressing whether risk is a component of the bundle of valued returns. If so, understanding how risk can be balanced against other returns could be important information for organizational decision makers. It might, for example, help decision makers anticipate the consequences of changing the risk level of a bundle of valued returns (Brown & Huber, 1992).

If we believe, as pundits keep telling us, that rapidly changing business environments are becoming the new reality, issues about uncertainty and risk will be even more important. However, important questions remained unanswered:

- What is risk? How it should be defined and measured? How do definitions of risk change when we are speaking about risk at the organization- versus individual-level?
- Do different sources of risk have different effects on compensation systems and managerial behaviors (Miller & Bromiley, 1990)?
- Does risk influence the composition of the bundle of valued returns? Must greater risk from one source (e.g. greater use of variable pay) be offset by lower risk in another (e.g. job security pledges)?

The behavioral issues are particularly important. We need to know more about how employees process risk in the employment relationship—especially risk related to pay and other employment returns, how perceptions of risk in the employment relationship are formed, and how these perceptions influence the relationships among compensation, behaviors, and attitudes.

The Politics of Pay

The literature on organizational politics indicates that attempts to manage impressions and influence important people may be more consequential than some would like to admit (Ferris & Judge, 1991). Ungson and Steers (1984) posit that CEO performance is, in part, dependent upon identifying, fostering, and maximizing strategic alliances with financial institutions, governments, and other key players. This political role is multifaceted; part diplomat, lobbyist, negotiator, sales person, and even figurehead, representing the company at important events. Lee Iacocca's ability to procure government loans to bail out Chrysler Motor Company is an example. These political roles may be as important as the decision-making responsibilities traditionally associated with senior management and, Ungson and Steers argue, are important determinants of managerial compensation. However, context, especially the organization's environment (industry, economics, international setting) likely has a lot to do with the relative importance of political roles. For example, political roles might be particularly important for organizations facing major challenges or threats. Executives of firms in the tobacco industry come to mind, as well as those in the banking and brokerage industries with the possible repeal of the Glass–Steagall Act. Ungson and Steers center their discussion on CEOs, but their framework could be applied to managers in general.

A very different approach to organizational politics is taken by Tosi and his colleagues (Gomez-Mejia, Tosi & Hinkin, 1987; Tosi & Gomez-Mejia, 1989, 1994; Werner & Tosi, 1995). Tosi's work focuses on the ability of owners to monitor and control managerial actions. These studies report distinct differences in compensation choices and outcomes between owner- and manager-controlled firms. Manager-controlled firms are those in which the company's stock is so widely held there is no single large stockholder who can exercise power over managers. In this case managers are able to exert excessive control over company decisions. The pay–performance link is much weaker in manager-controlled firms which indicates these managers are able to influence the performance contingency of their pay (Gomez-Mejia, Tosi & Hinkin, 1987). This extra control may allow managers to engage in other activities which enhance their compensation, but are simultaneously detrimental to their organizations (Amihud & Lev, 1981; Walsh & Seward, 1990). Westphal and Zajac (1994) used political theories to explain the paradoxical adoption of long-term CEO incentive plans that are not put into actual use. When managers have excessive control they may also be able to manipulate their company's board of directors (BOD) (Lambert, Larcker & Weigelt, 1993; Walsh & Seward, 1990; Westphal & Zajac, 1994). For example, the number of BOD members appointed by the CEO may be positively related to the CEO's ability to manipulate his or her compensation and that of other senior executives (Crystal, 1991; Lambert, Larcker & Weigelt, 1993). This research is complementary to Tosi's because it depicts managers as willing to manipulate their income through political means.

It appears that managers in manager-controlled firms may have greater opportunities to exercise excessive control on their own behalf and to the organization's detriment. Research needs to identify contextual conditions under which managers are more (or less) likely to use this power to their own advantage. One of the important consequences of this research is that it indicates behavioral theories can explain variance in managerial compensation not accounted for by economic theories. It also highlights limitations of the segmented proliferation of compensation theories and the need to expand our theoretical purview to include cross-disciplinary developments.

The Changing Workforce: Compensating Contingent Managers

Transferring work from permanent, full-time workers to contingent or contract workers, called externalization, seems to be increasing (Belous,

1989; Davis-Blake & Uzzi, 1993; Pfeffer & Baron, 1988). Externalization may have profound effects on the work performed by managers. Companies are shifting more work to contingent workers to avoid the costs associated with permanent workers (e.g., screening, selecting, hiring, training, and promotion expenses) and gain the ability to adjust workforce levels quickly at little direct expense (Davis-Blake & Uzzi, 1993; Pfeffer and Baron, 1988). Contingent workers are usually paid on a different, often lower, salary schedule compared with similar core (i.e., permanent, full-time) workers. Benefits and employment security also differ. There may, however, be a dark side to externalization. Differences in compensation may increase internal pay inequalities. Contingent workers may be less committed to organizational objectives, either to compensate for their different bundle of valued returns or because they lack loyalty to the organization (Kidwell & Bennett, 1993; Pfeffer, 1994). If core and contingent employees must work interdependently, such inequalities may lead to increased conflict (Davis-Blake & Uzzi, 1993; Harrison & Bluestone, 1990; Pfeffer & Davis-Blake, 1992).

Contingent workers are not a homogeneous group. They differ not only in their knowledge, skills, and abilities, but also in the type of employment relationship they desire. Handy (1990) suggests that not all contingent workers seek core worker status. Some people appear to be more committed to their field than their organization and may prefer a more flexible contingent status (Meyer, Allen & Smith, 1993). The bundle of valued returns necessary to induce desired behaviors from these workers is likely to be different. At a company located in Ithaca, New York, a wife–husband team share the job of Personnel Manager, each working part of the day and assuming a portion of the responsibilities. The notion of a flexible compensation scheme, analogous to a flexi-benefit plan, may fit with organizations employing a significant proportion of contingent workers, especially if they cut across functional roles and organizational levels. Furthermore, beyond the conventional core–contingent dichotomy, all employees are in some sense contingent. Contingent becomes a matter of degrees—the employment relation is a continuum of more to less contingent. One end of this continuum is represented by General Electric whose CEO Welch asserts "the new psychological contract, if there is such a thing, is that jobs at GE are the best in the world for people who are willing to compete". Such employability is clearly different from GE's competitors, such as Toshiba or Hyundai, who offer careers and more long-term, if not lifetime, employment relationships. The contingent nature of the employment relationship becomes part of the bundle of valued returns.

Very little is known about the outcomes of contingent employment relationships or the effects of mixing core and contingent workers.

Anecdotal evidence is our primary information source. Compensation issues, particularly those related to the bundle of valued returns, are a primary differentiating factor between the two groups of workers. As such, we need to learn more about how differences in compensation policies affect the outcomes of these two forms of employment relationships.

- Do all managerial and professional workers aspire to become core workers?
- Is the contingent contractual relationship a valued return for some managers?
- Does the inequality in employment relationships between core and contingent workers cause increased conflict, shirking, or even sabotage (McLean Parks & Kidder, 1994)? If so, what type of bundle would mitigate such behaviors?

Right now answers are based on speculation and conjecture, the state of knowledge is very incomplete and the research opportunity is great.

The Globalization of Compensation

Inuits allegedly have 200 words for snow, presumably reflecting its importance in their culture. US managers may have over 200 words for pay (Fay, 1989), perhaps reflecting its importance in their culture. Fundamental cultural differences influence the lens through which people view compensation. This is echoed in the different meanings compensation has in different languages. For example, the term for pay in Malaysia *ganti rugi* and in Slovak *kompenzácia* means to replace a loss; in Hebrew *shaceer* means reward, in Sweden *utjämnig* means making equal; and an early use of the word 'pay' in the English language meant to pacify or please (Remick, 1995; Shipley, 1984).

Culture, a learned system of meaning and values, exerts significant influence on work-related attitudes and behaviors (Bhagat, Kedia, Crawford & Kaplan, 1990; Hofstede, 1980; Triandis, 1993). Differences in cultural values most likely influence the basic premises underlying compensation theories, yet only two of the theories in Figure 2.1 (i.e., social and psychological contracts) explicitly include the role of norms and values. Theories of cultural values suggest that the saliency and value of employment returns are influenced by culture (Bhagat et al, 1990; Triandis, 1993). However, little is known about *how* culture influences the way people view their employment relationships and the returns they receive. Kim, Park and Suzuki (1990) report that the equity norm is held by employees from Japan, Korea, and the US, but the strength of the norm appears to vary across cultures. Hui, Triandis and Yee (1991) found that cultural differences explained when people used equity- or equality-based reward distributions, but the social situation also seems to influence how rewards are distributed. This raises the point that *intra*-cultural variation in equity norms may be greater than *inter*-cultural variation. We simply do not know. How these differences play out in the employment relationship is not well understood, but this research does indicate that cultural differences appear to affect attitudes about compensation. Once again a reoccurring theme emerges: controlling for context is of paramount importance. The effectiveness of international compensation policies must, at least in part, depend upon how they support or conflict with cultural norms and values (Arvey, Bhagat & Salas, 1991; Bhagat et al, 1990; Triandis, 1993). Understanding which cultural values matter and how they affect employees is profoundly important to managers as the globalization of economies continues.

One of Hofstede's (1980; Hofstede, Neuijen, Ohayv & Sanders, 1990) five dimensions of culture, individualism-collectivism, has a well developed theoretical and research literature and seems well suited to compensation research (see Wagner, 1995 for a review). Individualistic cultures value achievement, competition, and individual over group goals. Equity norms guide the allocation of rewards. Collectivist cultures emphasize security, conformity, and group over individual goals (Triandis, 1993; Wagner, 1995). The I–C dimension was used by Hui, Triandis and Yee (1991) in their study of reward distribution preferences. Theory predicts that individuals from collectivist cultures prefer equality-based distributions while those from individualist cultures prefer an equity basis (Hofstede, 1980; Triandis, 1993). This rather straightforward hypothesis is still understudied. The supply of research questions expands greatly when one considers that several dimensions of culture may work together to influence key compensation relationships, for example I–C and uncertainty avoidance (UA) (Hofstede, 1980; Triandis, 1993). Managers from a culture high on collectivism and UA may react more negatively to incentive pay than those from a high individualism/low UA culture. Whether these differences affect the pay–performance relation is not known. Cultural differences might also influence which components in the bundle of valued returns are salient and how various bundles influence work attitudes and behaviors.

There has also been limited exploration into the effects of expatriate compensation on managers' attitudes and behaviors. Expatriates are managers working in a country different from their native home. The considerable expatriate pay literature is mainly descriptive and prescriptive (Reynolds, 1994), little is known about the causes or consequences of expatriate compensation. Expatriate pay is unique in that it is designed, administered, and communicated as a "bundle of valued returns". Typical elements include base plus performance pay, allowances for housing and dependent education, tax equalization, relocation expenses, and premiums for international service. Research suggests that expatriates are sensitive to any changes in the elements of their bundle of valued returns (Guzzo, Noonan & Elron, 1994). More needs to be learned about the expatriate employment relationship and the role of the bundle of valued returns in it.

There are also global public policies differences. Some returns are taxed heavily in one country, but not in another. There are differences in caps on retirement plan contributions and regulations on the ratio of pay between the topmost and lowest organization levels in some countries, but not in others. What do compensation theories predict will occur under these conditions? Will the importance of non-cash returns in the bundle increase? As the move towards globalization continues, these research issues will gain in importance.

UNRESOLVED QUESTIONS ABOUT HIERARCHIES AND QUALITY IN PAY

There is an unexplored yet crucial disagreement over the structure of pay differences within an organization: should pay structures (differentials) be compressed and egalitarian or should they be consecutively larger like prizes in a golf tournament (Milkovich & Newman, 1993)? Tournament theory suggests the latter (Lazear & Rosen, 1981). Employees are motivated, tournament theorists argue, not only by their current level of compensation, but also by pay at higher levels in the organizational hierarchy. Like the prizes in a sports tournament, increasingly wider gaps between adjacent levels in the organizational hierarchy are posited to be motivating. Since *relative* performance matters, higher performing managers should garner a larger share of the compensation pie. Data from auto racing (Becker & Huselid, 1992) and professional golf (Ehrenberg & Bognanno, 1990) indicate that tournament structures are important for explaining individual performance. Proponents of more egalitarian pay, on the other hand, argue that managers find tournaments unfair and demotivating (Kochan & Osterman, 1994; Lawler, 1992; Pfeffer, 1994). Egalitarian pay structures (e.g., equal differentials) are said to inculate feelings of fairness, community, cooperation and team work (Kochan & Osterman, 1994; Pfeffer, 1994). While research contrasting the effects of different structures is rare, Cowherd and Levine (1992) report that the relative difference between top and lower-level employees' salaries is negatively related to product quality.

A key notion in both tournament and egalitarian models is that top managerial pay affects the attitudes and behaviors of employees throughout the organization. Whether through trickle down or more directly, the relative amount managers are paid influences their own motivation as well as that of other employees. The question is, "Do the behavioral premises underlying the egalitarian and hierarchical models hold—and in what contexts?" Virtually all of the research in support of tournaments has sampled work where only individual relative performance matters; there are no work interdependencies.[2] Where work is more highly interdependent, the competition among managers for higher pay fostered by tournament structures may be deleterious. Managerial cooperation appears to be related to the way managers are paid (Hill, Hitt & Hoskisson, 1992). On the other hand, compressed pay structures are believed to demotivate those at the top; the skills and effort required in upper level work are inequitably compensated compared to lower level work (Milkovich & Newman, 1996). So organizations with compressed pay structures may be beset by poorly performing senior decision makers or adverse selection ratios for top management positions. Whether and when tournaments are viewed as fair/unfair or egalitarian pay structures are viewed as just/unjust are questions yet to be answered. These theories are also silent about the effects of differences in *how* managers are paid. For example, does the degree to which senior management's pay is tied to organizational performance *vis-à-vis* lower levels make any difference? Other compensation theories (e.g., agency and expectancy theories) place great emphasis on the performance-contingency of pay. Perhaps if managers' pay is more dependent on organizational performance, other employees will perceive the differentials to be fair even though managers are paid relatively more. In other words, justice perceptions might be another important mitigating factor.

Survey evidence indicates that structures clearly vary within industries in the US and across countries (Milkovich & Newman, 1996). The ratio of top executive's pay to that of the lowest level worker is 120–150:1 in the US, 20–30:1 in Europe, and 15–20:1 in Japan (Crystal, 1991). In some countries the ratios are regulated by public policy. Again, context (e.g., public policy) plays an important role in understanding

---

[2] We recognize the important contributions of caddies to the performance of professional golfers and pit crews to the performance of auto racers. However, caddie and pit crew pay was not included in the studies cited above.

different configurations of the bundle of valued returns and their consequences. In the next section we examine public policy in terms of social contracts.

THE SOCIAL CONTRACT

Theories about the social contract—norms about fair treatment, justice, and rights—are among the oldest models applied to work (Locke, 1960/1962; Marx, 1906/1976; Rousseau, 1762/1962). While theories about the social contract may differ in specifics, most share common fundamentals. First, social contract theory stands in opposition to the assumption of opportunism (Williamson, 1985). Cooperation is assumed to be the fundamental motivation behind collective behavior; managers are expected to collaborate since organizational and individual success are inherently intertwined (Keeley, 1988; Lessnoff, 1990; Macneil, 1980).

Second, the social contract is posited to underlie all individual employment contracts; it carries societal norms into the work relationship. Societal norms about ethics, fair dealing, individual rights, and "due reward[s] in accordance with honor, standards, or law" (*The American Heritage Dictionary*, 3rd edn, p.979) influence the nature and structure of employment relations (Donaldson & Dunfee, 1994; Macneil, 1980; Schein, 1980).

> Contract without common needs and tastes created only by society is inconceivable. Contract between totally isolated, utility-maximizing individuals is not contract, but war . . . contract without social structure and stability is—quite literally—rationally unthinkable, just as man [sic] outside society is rationally unthinkable. (Macneil, 1980, p. 1).

Social and psychological contracts are distinct. A psychological contact is inherently an individual-level construct, encompassing the relationship between a single manager and a specific organization. A social contract governs the roles and responsibilities of the larger society—it affects and is affected by governmental bodies, public policies, organizations, and individuals. Social contract theories tell us what "ought" to occur in any employment relationship. The focus is frankly normative, reminding us that,

> no amount of empirical accuracy, including an infinite array of facts, can ever itself add up to form an "ought". . . . To suppose that one can deduce an "ought" from an "is", or, what amounts to the same thing, that one can deduce a normative ethical conclusion from empirical research, is to commit a logical mistake. (Donaldson & Dunfee, 1994, p. 253)

Third, the social contract dictates that all stakeholders in the organization must share fairly in organizational success; benefits from any collective action should be distributed in a just manner to all participants (Donaldson, 1990; Griesinger, 1990). The basis for this distribution may differ across social contracts (e.g., equity vs equality), nevertheless, justice norms dictate that no one should garner a disproportionate share of the benefits. "As some people improve their situations, others should continue to improve, to become better off" (Rawls, 1971/1990).

Donaldson (1990) discusses social contract issues under the rubric of stewardship theory and juxtaposes it with agency theory assumptions. According to Donaldson (1990), under stewardship theory the employer–employee relationship is one of cooperation; under agency theory it is one of conflict driven by opportunism. Under stewardship theory, organizational control mechanisms are directed at encouraging or unencumbering collaborative action; under agency theory organizational controls (contracts) are implemented to limit conflict or coerce joint effort. These contrasts raise some interesting research opportunities.

The organizational literature is witnessing a resurgent interest in trust as a differentiating factor in employment relationships (Kochan & Osterman, 1994; Pfeffer, 1994; Smith, 1992). Social contract theories offer a guide to analyzing the importance, development, and operation of trust in work relationships (Macneil, 1980, 1985). When there is a need for flexibility, where information is limited, or where conditions are in a state of flux, employment relationships cannot be specified in terms of a written contract (Macneil, 1980). Too many issues and contingencies would need to be covered and the difficulty in writing and enforcing such contracts makes them untenable. The alternative is to base the relationship on trust. Contractual solidarity results from interdependencies between organizations and managers; both parties recognize there is a strong need for future cooperation. Trust, then, ensures both parties will act to preserve the relationship. Psychological contracts theory adopts many of these presumptions and applies them to understanding how social norms prevade and influence managerial attitudes and behaviors (McLean Parks & Kidder, 1994; Rousseau & Parks, 1993; Schein, 1980).

Finally, there are public policies implications of social contracts. The public policies of representative governments theoretically reflect social contract norms. As such, they impose constraints on the employment relationship (e.g., minimum wage, social security, and family leave statutes). Expectations embedded in the psychological contract are probably influenced by public policy and policy debates. For example, recent criticisms of CEO pay may be changing managers' views of what are fair pay differentials in managerial ranks (and underlies our earlier discussion of hierarchical and egalitarian pay structures). The effects of differences in public policies on managers' expectations, the configuration of the bundle of valued returns, and its consequences is unknown. For example, differences in tax and family leave policies in the European Union may impact managerial attitudes toward the variable pay initiatives undertaken by many US-based multinationals. Since research applying the social contract view to the employment relationship is just beginning, opportunities abound.

SUMMARY

Paradoxically, change is becoming a constant in business. In a world where a variety of forces (some of which we discussed) create an almost constantly shifting setting for employment relationships, we believe that what is meant by compensation needs to be reconsidered. We have suggested the bundle of valued returns as a viable starting point. Given a definition of compensation that may include relational as well as economic aspects, we believe that it is important to understand contextual factors which may mitigate the compensation–attitude/ behavior–performance nexus. In our presentation, we used *practice* to inform us about contextual variables that matter and then turned back to *theory* to predict the potential implications and consequences of those factors. This process highlights that theory and research need to both inform managers' decisions and, in turn, to be informed by the consequences of those decisions. Ours is a field of inquiry irrevocably intertwined with the decisions of practical people.

As Mahoney (1979) points out, managerial compensation lacks a unifying theory. Indeed, we believe it is becoming increasingly segmented theoretically. One way around this segmentation might be a focus on compensation in context; understanding how environmental, organizational, and individual contexts influence the configuration and consequences of the bundle of valued returns (Figure 2.2). The multiple stakeholders to the employment relationship—societies, governments, economies, organizations, families, managers—create the contexts in which compensation systems operate. We illustrated how three such factors might operate.

- Risk at the individual (e.g., manager's preference for risk), organizational (e.g., financial stability of the organization), and environmental (e.g., industry-wide economic conditions) levels is important to theories on both sides of Figure 2.1. It may influence the relative weight given to performance-contingent pay in the bundle of valued returns, the necessary arrangement of other returns in an incentive-laden bundle, and the way managers react to the variable components of a particular bundle.

- Internal and external politics may operate at the individual (e.g., impression management), organizational (e.g., manipulating corporate governance mechanisms), and environmental (e.g., influencing the decisions of public policy makers) levels. Political factors may impact how much control managers have over their pay or the severity of restrictions imposed on the bundle by government regulations.

- Workforce changes appear to be occurring at the individual (e.g., what the manager wants out of the employment relationship), organizational (e.g., organization's core-contingent mix), and environmental (e.g., public policies regulating the employment relationship) levels. Such changes may be reflected in what returns a manager values, what type of employment exchange the manager wants, or what returns an organization is legally required to provide.

Obviously we encourage more research attention to these contextual variables themselves and, as our discussion of pay hierarchies was intended to illustrate, how they influence substantive areas of compensation research.

It is a challenging time in the field of managerial compensation. There is no shortage of practical innovations or research ideas. Yet, in this flow of innovations and ideas there may be opportunity. A blend of theory, research, and practice holds the promise of expanding knowledge about the forces and processes that shape compensation systems and their links with managers and organizations. Dunnette (1990) calls this the "blend that binds" because collaboration between scientists and practitioners may offer the best opportunity to enhance the effectiveness of both parties. We issue the same call, for a new partnership between managers and scholars to better advance the state of the field and facilitate our understanding of the critical role compensation plays in the employment relationship.

ACKNOWLEDGMENTS

The authors want to thank Charles Trevor for his helpful comments on the manuscript of this chapter.

REFERENCES

Amihud, Y. & Lev, B. (1981) Risk reduction as a managerial motive for conglomerate mergers. *Bell Journal of Economics*, **20**, 605—617.

Amit, R. & Wernerfelt, B. (1990) Why do firms reduce business risk? *Academy of Management Journal*, **33**, 520–533.

Arvey, R. D., Bhagat, R. S. & Salas, E. (1991) Cross-cultural and cross-national issues in personnel and human resources management: Where do we go from here? In K. M. Rowland & G. R. Ferris (Eds), *Research in Personnel and Human Resource Management* (vol. 9, pp. 367–407). Greenwich, CT: JAI Press.

Baker, G. P., Jensen, M. C. & Murphy, K. J. (1988) Compensation and incentives: Practice versus theory. *The Journal of Finance*, **33**, 593–616.

Barney, J. B. (1990) The debate between traditional management theory and organizational economics. *Academy of Management Review*, **15**, 382–393.

Barringer, M. A. & Milkovich, G. T. (1995) *Changing employing contracts: The relative effects of proposed changes in compensation, benefits, and employment security on employee outcomes.* Working paper 95-14. Ithaca, NY: Center for Advanced Human Resource Studies.

Beatty, R. P. & Zajac, E. J. (1994) Managerial incentives, monitoring, and risk bearing: A study of executive compensation, ownership and board structure in initial public offerings. *Administrative Science Quarterly*, **39**, 313–335.

Becker, B. E. & Huselid, M. A. (1992) The incentive effects of tournament compensation systems. *Administrative Science Quarterly*, **37**, 336–350.

Belous, R. S. (1989) How human resource systems adjust to the shift toward contingent workers. *Monthly Labor Review*, **112**, 7–12.

Bhagat, R. S., Kedia, B. L., Crawford, S. E. & Kaplan, M. R. (1990) Cross-cultural issues in organizational psychology: Emergent trends and directions for research in the 1990s. In C. L. Cooper & I. T. Robertson (Eds), *International Review of I/O Psychology* (vol. 5, pp. 9–99). Chichester, UK: John Wiley.

Bloom, M. C. (1996) *Using the contract metaphor to understand the bundle of returns in the employment relationship,* Unpublished doctoral dissertation, Cornell University, Ithaca, NY.

Bloom, M. C. & Milkovich, G. T. (1995) *The relationship between risk, performance-based pay, and organizational performance,* Working Paper #95-01, Ithaca, NY: Center for Advanced Human Resource Studies.

Bromiley, P. & Curley, S. P. (1992) Individual differences in risk taking. In J. F. Yates (Ed.), *Risk-taking Behavior* (pp. 87–132). New York: John Wiley.

Brown, K. A. & Huber, V. L. (1992) Lowering floors and raising ceilings: A longitudinal assessment of the effects of an earnings-at-risk plan on pay satisfaction. *Personnel Psychology*, **45**, 279–311.

Campbell, J. T. (1990) The role of theory in industrial and organizational psychology. In M. D. Dunnette & L. M. Hough (Eds), *Handbook of Industrial and Organizational Psychology* (2nd edn, vol. 1, pp. 39–73). Palo Alto, CA: Consulting Psychologists Press.

Cantor, N. (1990) From thought to behavior: "Having" and "doing" in the study of personality and cognition. *American Psychologist*, **45**, 735–750.

Cappelli, P. & Rogovsky, N. (1994) New work systems and skill requirements. *International Labour Review*, **133**, 205–220.

Cappelli, P. & Singh, H. (1992) Integrating strategic human resources and strategic management. In D. Lewin, O. S. Mitchell & P. D. Sherer (Eds), *Research Frontiers in Industrial Relations and Human Resources* (pp. 165–192).

Maddison, WI: Industrial Relations Research Association.

Cowherd, D. M. & Levine, D. I. (1992) Product quality and pay equity between lower-level employees and top management: An investigation of distributive justice theory. *Administrative Science Quarterly*, **37**, 302–320.

Crystal, G. S. (1991) *In Search of Excess: The Overcompensation of American Executives*. New York: Norton.

Davis-Blake, A. & Uzzi, B. (1993) Determinants of employment externalization: A study of temporary workers and independent contractors. *Administrative Science Quarterly*, **38**, 195–223.

Donaldson, L. (1990) The ethereal hand: Organizational economics and management theory. *Academy of Management Review*, **15**, 369–381.

Donaldson, T. & Dunfee, T. W. (1994) Toward a unified conception of business ethics: Integrative social contracts theory. *Academy of Management Review*, **19**, 252–284.

Drucker, P. (1992) *Managing for the Future*. New York: Dutton.

Dunnette, M. D. (1990) Blending the science and practice of industrial and organizational psychology: Where are we and where are we going? In M. D. Dunnette & L. M. Hough (Eds), *Handbook of Industrial and Organizational Psychology* (2nd edn, vol. 1, pp. 1–27). Palo Alto, CA: Consulting Psychologists Press.

Ehrenberg, R. G. & Bognanno, M. L. (1990) The incentive effects of tournaments revisited: Evidence from the European PGA tour. *Industrial and Labor Relations Review*, **43**, 74-S–88-S.

Ehrenberg, R. G. & Smith, R. (1991) *Modern Labor Economics: Research and Public Policy*. New York: Harper Collins.

Eisenberger, R., Faslo, P. & Davis-LaMastro, V. (1990) Perceived organizational support and employee diligence, commitment and innovation. *Journal of Applied Psychology*, **75**, 51–59.

Eisenberger, R., Huntington, R., Hutchison, S. & Sowa, D. (1986) Perceived organizational support. *Journal of Applied Psychology*, **71**, 500–507.

Eisenhardt, K. M. (1989) Agency theory: An assessment and review. *Academy of Management Review*, **14**, 57–74.

Fay, C. F. (1989) *Glossary of Compensation and Benefits Terms*, Scottsdale, AZ: American Compensation Association.

Ferris, G. R. & Judge, T. A. (1991) Personnel/Human Resources Management: A political influence perspective. *Journal of Management*, **17**, 447–488.

Gerhart, B. & Milkovich, G. T. (1993) Employee compensation: Research and Theory. In M. D. Dunnette & L. M. Hough (Eds), *Handbook of Industrial and Organizational Psychology* (2nd edn, vol. 3, pp. 481–569). Palo Alto, CA: Consulting Psychologists Press.

Gomez-Mejia, L. R. & Balkin, D. (1992) *Compensation, Organizational Strategy, and Firm Performance*. Cincinnati, OH: Southwestern Publishing.

Gomez-Mejia, L. R., Tosi, H. & Hinkin, T. (1987) Managerial control, performance, and executive compensation, *Academy of Management Journal*, **30**, 51–70.

Griesinger, D. W. (1990) The human side of economic organization. *Academy of Management Review*, **15**, 478–499.

Guzzo, R. A., Noonan, K. A. & Elron, E. (1994) Expatriate managers and the psychological contract. *Journal of Applied Psychology*, **79**, 617–626.

Hammer, M. & Champy, J. (1993) *Reengineering the Corporation: A Manifesto for Business Revolution*. New York: Harper Business.

Handy, C. (1990) *The Age of Unreason*, Boston: Harvard Business School Press.

Harrison, B. & Bluestone, B. (1990) Wage polarization in the US and the "flexibility debate". *Cambridge Journal of Economics, 14*, 351–373.

Heilbroner, R. L. (1986) *The Worldly Philosophers: The Lives, Times and Ideas of the Great Economic Thinkers*. New York: Touchstone.

Hill, C. W., Hitt, M. A. & Hoskisson, R. E. (1992) Cooperative versus competitive structures in related and unrelated diversified firms. *Organization Science, 3*, 501–521.

Hofstede, G. (1980) *Culture's Consequences: International Differences in Work-related Values*, Beverly Hills, CA: Sage Publications.

Hofstede, G., Neuijen, B., Ohayv, D. D. & Sanders, G. (1990) Measuring organizational cultures: A qualitative and quantitative study across twenty cases. *Administrative Science Quarterly, 35*, 286–316.

Hoskisson, R. E., Hitt, M. A., Turk, T. A. & Tyler, B. B. (1989) Balancing corporate strategy and executive compensation: Agency theory and corporate governance. In K. M. Rowland & G. R. Ferris (Eds), *Research in Personnel and Human Resource Management* (vol. 7, pp. 25–57). Greenwich, CT: JAI Press.

Hui, C. H., Triandis, H. C. & Yee, C. (1991) Cultural differences in reward allocation: Is collectivism the explanation? *British Journal of Social Psychology, 30*, 145–157.

Huselid, M. A. (1995) The impact of human resource management practices on turnover productivity, and financial performance. *Academy of Management Journal, 38*, 635–672.

Jackson, S. E. & Schuler, R. S. (1995) Understanding human resource management in the context of organizations and their environments. *Annual Review of Psychology, 46*, 237–264.

James, L. R., Demaree, R. G., Mulaik, S. A. & Ladd, R. T. (1992) Validity generalization in the context of situational models. *Journal of Applied Psychology, 77*, 3–14.

James, L. R. & James, L. A. (1992) Psychological climate and affect. In C. J. Cranny, P. C. Smith & E. F. Stone (Eds), *Job Satisfaction: How People Feel About their Jobs and How It Affects their Performance*, New York: Lexington Books.

Kahneman, D., Slovic, P. & Tversky, A. (1982) *Judgment under Uncertainty: Heuristics and Biases*. London: Cambridge University Press.

Kanfer, R. (1990) Motivation theory and industrial and organizational psychology. In M. D. Dunnette & L. M. Hough (Eds), *Handbook of Industrial and Organizational Psychology* (2nd edn, vol. 1, pp. 75–170). Palo Alto, CA: Consulting Psychologists Press.

Keeley, M. (1988) *A Social-Contract Theory of Organizations*. South Bend, IN: University of Notre Dame Press.

Kidwell, R. E., Jr & Bennett, N. (1993) Employee propensity to withhold effort: A conceptual model to intersect three avenues of research. *Academy of Management Review, 18*, 429–456.

Kim, K. I., Park, H. & Suzuki, N. (1990) Reward allocations in the United States, Japan, and Korea: A comparison of individualistic and collectivistic cultures. *Academy of Management Journal, 33*, 188–198.

Kochan, T. A. & Osterman, P. (1994) *The Mutual Gains Enterprise: Forging a Winning Partnership Among Labor, Management, and Government*. Boston: Harvard Business School Press.

Lambert, R. A., Larcker, D. F. & Weigelt, K. (1993) The structure of organizational incentives. *Administrative Science Quarterly, 38*, 438–461.

Lawler, E. E. (1971) *Pay and Organizational Effectiveness: A Psychological View.* New York: McGraw-Hill.

Lawler, E. E. (1992) *The Ultimate Advantage: Creating the High-Involvement Organization.* San Francisco: Jossey-Bass.

Lazear, E. & Rosen, S. (1981) Rank-order tournaments as optimum labor contracts. *Journal of Political Economy,* **89,** 841–864.

Lessnoff, M. (Ed.) (1990) *Social Contract Theory.* Washington Square, NY: New York University Press.

Levinthal, D. (1988) A survey of agency models of organizations. *Journal of Economic Behavior and Organizations,* **9,** 153–185.

Locke, J. (1960/1962) An essay concerning the true original extent and end of civil government. In E. Baker (Ed.), *Social Contract: Essays by Locke, Hume, and Rousseau.* New York: Oxford University Press.

Lopes, L. L. (1987) Between hope and fear. *Advances in Experimental Social Psychology,* **20,** 255–295.

Macneil, I. R. (1980) *The New Social Contract.* New Haven, CT: Yale University Press.

Macneil, I. R. (1985) Relational contract: What we do and do not know. *Wisconsin Law Review,* 483–525.

Mahoney, T. A. (1979) *Compensation and Reward Perspectives.* Homewood, IL: Richard D. Irwin.

March, J. G. & Simon, H. A. (1958) *Organizations.* New York: John Wiley.

Marx, K. (1906/1976) *Capital.* Harmondsworth: Penguin.

McLean Parks, J. & Kidder, D. L. (1994) "Till death us do part . . ." changing work relationships in the 1990s. In C. L. Cooper & D. M. Rousseau (Eds), *Trends in Organizational Behavior* (vol. 1, pp. 111–136). New York: John Wiley.

Meyer, J. P., Allen, N. J. & Smith, C. A. (1993) Commitment to organizations and occupations: Extension and test of a three-component conceptualization. *Journal of Applied Psychology,* **78,** 538–551.

Miceli, M. P. & Lane, M. C. (1991) Antecedents of pay satisfaction: A review and extension. In K. M. Rowland & G. R. Ferris (Eds) *Research in Personnel and Human Resource Management* (vol. 9, pp. 235–309). Greenwich, CT: JAI Press.

Milkovich, G. T. & Newman, J. M. (1993) *Compensation* (4th edn). Homewood, IL: Irwin.

Milkovich, G. T. & Newman, J. M. (1996) *Compensation* (5th edn). Homewood, IL: Irwin.

Miller, K. & Bromiley, P. (1990) Strategic risk and corporate performance: An analysis of alternative risk measures. *Academy of Management Journal,* **33,** 759–779.

Opsahl, R. L. & Dunnette, M. D. (1966) The role of financial compensation in industrial motivation. *Psychological Bulletin,* **66,** 94–118.

Osterman, P. (1988) *Employment Futures.* New York: Oxford University Press.

Pfeffer, J. (1994) *Competitive Advantage through People: Unleashing the Power of the Workforce.* Boston: Harvard Business School Press.

Pfeffer, J. & Baron, J. N. (1988) Taking the workers back out: Recent trends in the structuring of employment. In L. Cummings & B. M. Staw (Eds), *Research in Organizational Behavior* (vol. 10, pp. 257–303). Greenwich, CT: JAI Press.

Pfeffer, J. & Davis, Blake, A. (1992) Salary dispersion, location in the salary distribution, and turnover among college administrators. *Industrial and Labor Relations Review,* **45,** 753–763.

Rawls, J. (1971/1990) Contractarian justice. In M. Lessnoff (Ed.), *Social Contract*

Theory (pp. 138–164). Washington Square, NY: New York University Press.

Remick, R. (1995) Pay and compensation: Different meanings to different people. Unpublished manuscript, Cornell University.

Reynolds, C. (1994) *Compensation Basics for North American Expatriates: Developing an Effective Program for Employees Working Abroad*. Scottsdale, AZ: American Compensation Association.

Rousseau, D. M. & Parks, J. M. (1993) The contracts of individuals and organizations. In L. L. Cummings & B. M. Staw (Eds), *Research in Organizational Behavior* (vol. 15, pp. 1–47). Greenwich, CT: JAI Press.

Rousseau, J. J. (1762/1962) An essay concerning the true original extent and end of civil government. In E. Baker (Ed.), *Social Contract: Essays by Locke, Hume, and Rousseau*. New York: Oxford University Press.

Schein, E. H. (1980) *Organizational Psychology* (3rd edn). Englewood Cliffs, NJ: Prentice-Hall.

Schneider, S. L. & Lopes, L. L. (1986) Reflection in preferences under risk: Who and when may suggest why. *Journal of Experimental Psychology: Human Perception and Performance*, **12**, 535–548.

Shipley, J. T. (1984) *Origins of English Words: A Discursive Dictionary of Indo-European Roots*. Baltimore, MD: Johns Hopkins University Press.

Simon, H. A. (1951) Formal theory of the employment relationship. *Econometrica*, **19**, 293–305.

Smith, A. (1776/1976) *An Inquiry into the Nature and Causes of the Wealth of Nations*. Dunwoody, GA: Norman S. Berg.

Smith, P. C. (1992) In pursuit of happiness: Why study general job satisfaction? In C. J. Cranny, P. C. Smith & E. F. Stone (Eds), *Job Satisfaction: How People Feel About their Jobs and How It Affects their Performance* (pp. 5–20). New York: Lexington Books.

Tosi, H. L., Jr & Gomez-Mejia, L. R. (1989) The decoupling of CEO pay and performance: An agency theory perspective. *Administrative Science Quarterly*, **34**, 169–190.

Tosi, H. L., Jr & Gomez-Mejia, L. R. (1994) CEO compensation monitoring and firm performance. *Academy of Management Journal*, **37**, 1002–1016.

Triandis, H. C. (1993) Cross-cultural industrial and organizational psychology. In H. C. Triandis, M. D. Dunnette & L. M. Hough (Eds), *Handbook of Industrial and Organizational Psychology* (2nd edn, vol. 4, pp. 103–172). Palo Alto, CA: Consulting Psychologists Press.

Tsui, A. S., Pearce, J. L., Porter, L. W. & Hite, J. P. (1995) Choice of employee–organization relationship: Influence of external and internal organization factors. In G. R. Ferris (Ed.), *Research in Personnel and Human Resource Management* (vol 13, pp. 117–151). Greenwich, CT: JAI Press.

Ungson, G. R. & Steers, R. M. (1984) Motivation and politics in executive compensation. *Academy of Management Review*, **9**, 313–323.

Wagner, J. A., III (1995) Studies of individualism-collectivism: Effects on cooperation in groups. *Academy of Management Journal*, **38**, 152–172.

Walsh, J. P. & Seward, J. K. (1990) On the efficiency of internal and external corporate control mechanisms. *Academy of Management Review*, **15**, 421–458.

Werner, S. & Tosi, H. L. (1995) Other people's money: effects of ownership on compensation strategy & executive pay. *Academy of Management Journal*, **38**, 1672–1691.

Westphal, J. D. & Zajac, E. J. (1994) Substance and symbolism in CEO's long-term incentive plans. *Administrative Science Quarterly*, **39**, 367–390.

Williamson, O. E. (1985) *The Economic Institutions of Capitalism*. New York: Free Press.

Wright, P. M., McMahan, G. C. & McWilliams, A. (1994) Human resources and sustained competitive advantage: A resource-based perspective. *International Journal of Human Resource Management*, **5**, 301–326.

Wright, P. M., Smart, D. & McMahan, G. C. (in press) On the integration of strategy and human resources: An investigation of the match between human resources and strategy among NCAA basketball teams. *Academy of Management Journal*.

CHAPTER 3

Employee Theft

Liane Greenberg and Julian Barling

Queen's University, Ontario, Canada

Employee theft remains a long-standing employee concern, and in some settings, it is commonplace. Employee theft occurs across all business domains; estimates of employees who steal vary from 28% of manufacturing workers to 33% of hospital employees, and 35%, 43%, and 62% of retail business employees (Hollinger & Clark, 1983a), supermarket employees, and fast food restaurant employees, respectively (Slora, 1989). With increasing social changes, more companies may be faced with theft as a result of jobs becoming temporary (McLean Parks & Kidder, 1994), and employees switching jobs and maintaining multiple careers (Tucker, 1989). Given the widespread nature of employee theft (Bales, 1988), and its consequences for consumers and employers, we need to understand it better in the hope of moving towards better control and possible prevention. Employee theft is of interest to us, not only as an activity that must be regulated or prevented, but because it indicates the health of the relationship between employer and employee.

In this chapter, we will discuss the problems with defining employee theft, the costs of employee theft, and finally, the causes and possible prevention of employee theft.

DEFINING AND MEASURING EMPLOYEE THEFT

There is little consistency across studies in the identification of different types of theft and in the definition of employee theft. For example, Hollinger and Clark (1983a) defined theft as "the unauthorized taking, control, or transfer of money and/or property of the formal work organization that is perpetrated by an employee during the course of

Trends in Organizational Behavior, Volume 3. Edited by C. L. Cooper and D. M. Rousseau

occupational activity" (p. 2). However, Slora (1989) distinguishes between production deviance and employee theft; production deviance includes activities which interfere with the rate or quality of output, while employee theft refers to the unauthorized taking of cash, merchandise, or property. In his review of employee theft, Caudill (1988) lists behaviors which he classifies as employee theft (e.g., taking unauthorized long lunch breaks, misusing sick leave, using alcohol or drugs in the workplace, industrial espionage, releasing confidential information, taking kickbacks and embezzling money). Typically, however, most other researchers would not include these behaviors in their definition. Instead, these behaviors are usually classified as production deviance. Hollinger, Slora and Terris (1992) have identified another type of theft, altruistic property deviance, which is defined as the giving away of company property to others, either at no charge or at a substantial discount, usually to improve social relationships with peers. Similarly, Hawkins (1984) reported that waiters commonly give away "free food to friends" (p. 56); he described this behavior as socially based theft. Instead of suggesting that there is only one definition of employee theft, therefore, perhaps a more appropriate approach would be to accept that employee theft takes many different forms which are both profuse in number and elaborate in design.

Employers and employees vary considerably in what they consider to be theft. The above behaviors may be considered to be theft by researchers but not by the "victims" (i.e., the organizations) or the "thieves" (i.e., the employees), or may be considered to be theft by the victims but not by the thieves. Taylor (1986) suggests that management may nominate a behavior as stealing if employees sell what they stole but not if they keep it for their personal use. Even employees who take company property (e.g., food) often do not view their own behavior as stealing; they will admit to eating food on the job but will not call it theft.

An even larger deterrent in defining theft is that it may be completely overlooked or ignored for several reasons. For example, employee theft might be perceived as managerial weakness by the public (Taylor, 1986), there may be no apparent solutions to prevent it (Taylor, 1986), organizations may believe erroneously that they are immune to employee theft (Caudill, 1988), or that it is not a major problem for them. Lastly, employee theft may be accepted as an unavoidable part of fixed operating costs, that is, a cost of doing business (Taylor, 1986).

The discussion so far demonstrates some of the obstacles to a consistent definition of employee theft. The lack of a consistent definition is one source of difficulty for obtaining accurate base rates of employee theft. Before organizations begin to tackle the problem of employee theft, its extent must be determined (Slora, 1989). Several different indices have been used. For example, using shrinkage (the unaccounted loss in dollars after sales reductions and unsold stock have been subtracted from initial inventories) to estimate internal theft is problematic because shrinkage can result from several different factors other than employee theft, such as shoplifting, misplaced merchandise, and bookkeeping errors. Similarly, using the number of employees apprehended as an indication of the extent of theft will not provide an accurate estimate because of the low base rate of such apprehensions. Anonymous surveys to collect self-report data on theft behavior (e.g., Hollinger & Clark, 1983a) have problems with unreported acts of theft because of the socially undesirable nature of this behavior, and employee self-perceptions that they are not thieves. Thus, the actual prevalence of employee theft is probably much higher than what is reported (Kamp & Brooks, 1991).

COSTS OF EMPLOYEE THEFT

Both organizations and consumers must contend with the consequences of employee theft. It has been estimated that employee theft results in an annual loss exceeding 40 billion dollars for American businesses (Palmiotto, 1983); ten times that of street crime (see Bacas, 1987). In fact, the greatest source of loss due to crimes against business comes from employee theft (American Management Association, 1977) making it the most expensive form of non-violet crime against business (Greenberg, 1990). Over and above an organization's potential losses in profits, is the more deleterious consequence of employee theft being a major factor in 20 to 30% of bankruptcies (American Management Association, 1977; Morgenstern, 1977). If this is indeed the case, all employees—including those who do not engage in employee theft—would be hurt as well. Lastly, customers and consumers suffer because prices inevitably rise to offset losses due to employee theft (Brown & Pardue, 1985).

The focus of this chapter now turns to two different theories accounting for the occurrence of employee theft, namely person theories and workplace theories. Thereafter, some theories and approaches to prevention and control will be considered.

PERSON THEORIES

Person-based theories attempt to explain why *some* people would pilfer from an organization; as such, they imply a consistency of behavior across both time and situations.

The Need Approach

The notion that employees steal from their organization because of their own financial needs is not new. Cressey (1953) posited that employees steal to resolve financial difficulties that have no conventional solutions (e.g., drug habits, gambling). Within this framework, people rely on illegitimate methods to achieve socially acceptable goals when external financial pressures become great (Merton, 1938). More recently, this theory has been criticized because it does not adequately explain the association between the type of the economic needs and how the stolen materials satisfy those needs (Hollinger & Clark, 1983a).

Social needs can also lead to employee theft for people with high belongingness needs, particularly if there is pressure from peers to steal. This may be especially relevant for young employees (Caudill, 1988). The social need theory could be extended to explain "altruistic deviance" (Hollinger, Slora & Terris, 1992) where employees give stolen goods to others so that they may be accepted by them.

Deviant Individual Backgrounds

Another current theory suggests that the propensity to engage in workplace theft is a function of deviant individuals. Proponents of the "deviant background" approach hold that if a consistent link can be demonstrated between certain attitudes and theft, there may be an underlying personality construct which can explain employee counterproductive behaviors, including employee theft. For example, a profile of the "typical" employee-thief would include being more tempted to steal, engaging more in rationalizations for theft, being prepared to punish other thieves less, thinking frequently about theft-related activities, attributing more theft to others, showing more loyalty to those guilty of employee theft, and being more vulnerable to peer pressure to steal (e.g., Terris & Jones, 1982). In one study, employees who were fired for counterproductive behaviors including theft were more likely to admit to past theft and scored significantly lower on an honesty scale (Jones, Joy, Werner & Orban, 1991).

Greed or Temptation (Opportunity)

This theory suggests that people are inherently greedy and that every employee would steal if given the chance (Astor, 1972; Lipman, 1973). Researchers who advocate this theory propose that greed will not translate into theft unless opportunities, which bring out the natural greed of employees, present themselves (e.g., misplaced trust with cash, records, keys and safe combinations). Opportunity certainly correlates positively with theft (Kantor, 1983; Lydon, 1984). This approach lends itself to theft-deterrence by minimizing opportunity (e.g., provide constant surveillance over employee activity, locking everything up).

"Epidemic of Moral Laxity"

Employee theft has also been attributed to an "epidemic of moral laxity", especially among younger members of the workforce (Merriam, 1977). This notion postulates that today's employees do not possess the same trustworthy qualities as employees of yesteryear. There is some support for this theory in that more theft involvement has been found among younger employees (Franklin, 1975; Hollinger & Clark, 1983b). However, the higher proportion of theft among employed youths can also be explained by alternative theories: they disproportionately occupy marginal positions (low status, minimal tenure, social isolation) and steal as a way to express grievances (Tucker, 1989), they manifest lower commitment to their employers (Hollinger, 1986), they are often dissatisfied with their employment experience (Hollinger & Clark, 1982), and they are not sufficiently deterred by the threat of existing formal or informal negative sanctions (Hollinger & Clark, 1983b). These alternative theories suggest that theft is more closely related to an employee's position in the organizational hierarchy, tenure, and dissatisfaction than it is to moral laxity, and that a thorough investigation of employee theft should consider the role of workplace predictors in addition to personal characteristics.

The Marginality Proposition

One popular explanation for employee theft is that the youth of today are morally lax. In contrast, as the marginality hypothesis suggests, it is not so much employees' age that is related to theft, but rather the nature of jobs that the youth of today often hold.

According to Tucker (1989), the underlying cause of theft of property is the employee's "degree of marginality". Marginal employees are characterized by their low status, low rank in the organizational hierarchy, low wages, expendability, little opportunity for advancement, short tenure, little chance to develop relationships, lack of security, and social isolation. Also, the temporary nature of work consistently emerges as important in distinguishing between high and low deviance involvement (Hollinger & Clark, 1983a; McLean Parks & Kidder, 1994; Robin, 1969). Temporary workers often have not had an opportunity for developing a commitment to a career with the organization (Hollinger,

1986) and have had little time to develop a relationship with their employer (Tucker, 1989). Temporary and contingent workers, who are increasing in number, should probably be included in this category because of their marginal status (Barling & Gallagher, in press; McLean Parks & Kidder, 1994).

Person theories have implications for reducing employee theft: They generally advocate prevention through personnel selection (or more accurately, through personnel exclusion). They focus on devices designed to discover employees who have tendencies to steal (e.g., paper and pencil honesty tests) once on the job, and presumably select the most honest and trustworthy employees from a pool of applicants (that is, screen out the potential thief).

WORKPLACE THEORIES

Person theories attempt to explain why some people would steal from an organization. In contrast, workplace-based theories attempt to explain why *specific* organizations might suffer higher levels of employee theft. In this way, workplace-based theories are situation-specific and result in a different set of strategies for understanding and controlling employee theft.

Organizational Climate

Kamp and Brooks (1991) suggest the existence of an "organizational theft" climate which can be either honest or dishonest in nature. An honest organizational theft climate would send messages to employees that theft was unacceptable. Supporting this notion, Kamp and Brooks (1991) found that employees' perceptions about management's attitudes to theft, and the attitudes of their immediate supervisor, their coworkers, and their own personal attitudes toward theft were related to employees' self-reported on-the-job theft. Support for this particular approach emanates from research showing that absenteeism is associated with perceptions of the organization's absence climate (Johns, 1987).

Deterrence Doctrine

Similar to the organizational climate theory of theft is the "deterrence doctrine" which holds that the perceived threat of organizational sanctions influences personal behavior (Gibbs, 1975). The essence of this approach is that employee theft will be more likely in an organization that does not make its anti-theft policies explicit. The deterrence process includes three major variables: perceived certainty (risk of being discovered), perceived severity (possible criminal justice punishment options), and visibility of punishment. Research indicates that it is the perceived certainty of punishment that is most effective in deterring theft (Tittle & Logan, 1973). Kantor (1983) suggests that a large number of employees will engage in employee theft if they see others doing so without being apprehended or punished. It follows that an organization must overtly show that they do not tolerate theft so as to prevent employees from stealing. The deterrence doctrine is supported by findings showing that the likelihood of males engaging in sexually harassing behavior is reduced significantly when they believe that the organization will invoke sanctions against such behavior (Dekker & Barling, 1995).

Perceived Organizational Fairness

Another explanatory model points to a relationship between employees' perceptions of organizational fairness and employee theft. In this respect, interpersonal and payment fairness have been associated with employee theft.

Several different researchers have noted that rather than considering theft a crime, it is better characterized as a mode of social counter-control (Black, 1987). Within this framework, employee theft is seen as a specific response to perceived deviant behavior of the employer (Tucker, 1989), perhaps even a way of getting back at the employer (Mars, 1982). As such, this theory demonstrates the "flipside" of the "theft by inherently bad employees" argument; it points to exploitation by the employer as a cause of pilferage. Although this phenomenon has not been directly studied, there is some empirical support for this theory. For example, Hollinger and Clark (1983a) found that the single best predictor of theft was employee attitudes and feelings of being exploited by the company or its officers. Similarly, job burnout and job dissatisfaction are associated with employees' admissions of theft (Clark & Hollinger, 1981).

A second form of perceived unfairness that can lead to feelings of dissatisfaction is payment inequity, which would arise when the rewards employees receive, relative to the work they are doing, are seen to be less than they should be. In that situation, employees are likely to respond in one of two ways (Adams, 1965): they could lower their inputs (e.g., job performance) or raise their outcomes (e.g., pay demands, employee theft). For example, when studying maritime dock workers, Mars (1974) discovered that employees engaging in theft viewed it "as a morally justified addition to wages . . . as an entitlement due from exploiting employers" (p. 244). Findings from more recent research sustain this argument. When pay cuts were perceived as unfair, they resulted in substantial employee theft and turnover. In contrast, when pay cuts of exactly the same magnitude were introduced in the same organization in a more informative and sensitive manner, employee theft and turnover were substantially lower (Greenberg, 1990, 1993). These findings will have important implications for intervention as well as future research.

INTERACTION OF PERSON AND WORKPLACE FACTORS

Because many factors contribute to an employee's decision to steal, a complete model of theft should include both person and workplace factors. This approach would be consistent with Bandura's (1977) social learning theory, as well as data showing that using an interaction of workplace and person factors provides a better prediction of both workplace aggression (Greenberg & Barling, 1995) and sexual harassment (Dekker & Barling, 1995).

It is believed that three factors must be present for an employee to steal (e.g., Bologna, 1980): opportunity (when employees believe there is little risk of being caught or punished, i.e., no deterrence), need (this factor is mostly the perception of need as opposed to a real need), and attitudes toward theft. Regardless of the presence of both opportunity and need, employee theft can be minimized when attitudes are clearly intolerant of such behavior (Brown & Pardue, 1985). An anecdotal study suggests that an employee's characteristics when entering an organization, organizational characteristics that directly or indirectly relate to theft, and the employee's emotional and intellectual reactions to these organizational characteristics all combine to result in theft behavior (Taylor, 1986).

The way in which personal and organizational factors predict employee theft independently is presented in Figure 3.1. In addition, some of the potential interactions between organizational and personal factors are also identified in Figure 3.1.

REDUCING OR PREVENTING EMPLOYEE THEFT

There are two main approaches to reducing the occurrences of employee theft: prevention and control. Prevention has been referred to as a bottom-up approach while control has been called a top-down approach.

Prevention of Employee Theft: Strategies from Person Theories

The person theories that explain why employees steal advocate prevention through personnel selection. Consistent with this approach,

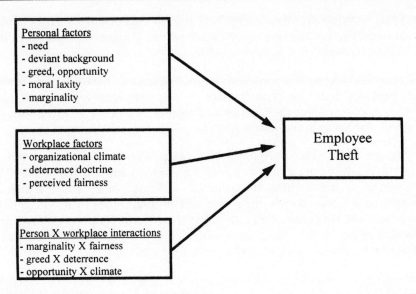

Figure 3.1   Predictors of employee theft

questionnaires are designed to discover applicants who have tendencies to steal, and once potential thieves are identified, they are excluded during the hiring process. The most often used methods of screening are background checks, employment interviews, polygraph examinations, and written integrity tests. Preemployment "paper-and-pencil" honesty tests, for example, have been suggested by some to be successful at identifying potential employee thieves (e.g., Jones, Slora & Boye, 1990; McDaniel & Jones, 1988). Polygraph tests (Terris & Jones, 1982) and investigations into past employers, credit bureaux, and police agencies (Owens, 1976; Willis, 1986) have also been claimed to be effective at discovering employees with propensities for theft.

Background check. –The underlying assumption for the background check is that a history of previous theft behavior predicts future theft. While seemingly uncomplicated, there are several limitations to this screening method.

- The majority of employee thieves are never caught.
- Even if employees are apprehended, they will often go unpunished. Thus, there would be no existing record of their theft because they were not formally charged.
- It is becoming increasingly difficult to obtain information about prior employment because of privacy legislation.

- There may be no relationship between an individual's theft behavior in two different organizations or across two different situations in the same organization (Greenberg, 1990).

Hence, choosing to hire someone because of the absence of a prior record of employee theft, or choosing not to hire someone because of prior instances of employee theft, could lead to a series of incorrect decisions. As a result, the background check is an unreliable tool for theft prevention.

Polygraph test. –The polygraph test, better known as the lie-detector, was frequently used as a screening instrument in the past. The polygraph is not without its faults; some limitations include a lack of standardized procedures in its use, and its high costs in terms of both time and effort (Terris, 1982). In 1988, the federal Employee Polygraph Protection Act in the United States banned the use of the polygraph as a selection tool in most areas of the private sector.

Employment interview. –Although the employment interview may be useful for narrowing down the choices for a job position, it should not be relied on as a method to identify employees who are likely to engage in counterproductive behavior in the workplace. Interviewers often rely on false criteria because of the lack of information concerning behaviors that might be associated with theft.

Honesty tests. –Another response to employee theft and its consequences has been increased efforts to detect dishonest job applicants through personality testing. The interest in, and use of paper and pencil honesty tests (or integrity tests) as a selection instrument have increased because of legislation prohibiting the use of the polygraph. Honesty tests are paper and pencil devices developed primarily to predict theft and other forms of dishonesty. Overt integrity tests typically contain self-report indices that inquire directly about the applicant's attitudes toward theft and violence, past theft involvement, and alcohol and drug use. These tests are based on the assumption that job applicants who are at high risk of stealing while on the job can be identified successfully. Once these potential thieves are identified, they can then be selected-out during the application/hiring process.

Some Advantages of Preemployment Testing

There is some support for the use of preemployment screening in reducing theft. In general, employee theft rates are lower in organizations which conduct careful and extensive preemployment screening (Baumer & Rosenbaum, 1984), and this has been replicated in supermarket chains (Jones, Slora & Boye, 1990), convenience stores (Terris & Jones, 1982) and retain drug chains (Brown & Pardue, 1985). Similarly, preselecting employees on the basis of honesty and integrity reduces subsequent terminations and prosecutions for employee theft (Hartnett, 1990). Thus, honesty tests are useful in reducing both the number of dishonest people in the workplace and the occurrences of employee theft, and in increasing the probability of hiring honest and dependable employees from a pool of applicants (Jones, Slora & Boye, 1990; Jones et al, 1991). One question that remains for future research is whether it is the honesty testing per se that affects employee theft, or whether organizations that engage in such practices implicitly construct an organizational theft culture that discourages employee theft (i.e. they send a message to employees that theft will not be tolerated).

Integrity tests can also be used to predict theft among current employees. Screening current employees also creates a "non-theft climate", and deters theft in that employees perceive their employers as taking theft very seriously (Jones & Terris, 1984).

Limitations of Preemployment Testing

Although integrity tests have been shown to predict on-the-job theft, they still need to be used with caution for several reasons:

- It is ironical and unreasonable to expect dishonest people to answer questions truthfully about their own attitudes toward theft and past dishonest behavior.
- Attitudes about theft or personality tendencies are only moderately correlated with theft behaviors.
- Opportunity for theft does not necessarily lead to greater occurrences of theft. In fact, most employees in various occupations have access to money or merchandise but choose not to steal (Hollinger & Clark, 1983a).
- Labelling someone a "thief" may become a self-fulfilling prophesy (Guastello & Rieke, 1991), and would certainly make it more difficult for that person to obtain alternative employment.
- Privacy issues (Guastello & Rieke, 1991).
- Most importantly, this approach ignores the potential contribution of workplace factors that might lead to employee theft.

Reducing Employee Theft: Strategies from Workplace Theories

These strategies differ from preselection in that they are concerned with theft by *current* employees in *specific* situations. To reduce employee theft, it is necessary to focus on redesigning the workplace. Several methods or techniques are consistent with this approach:

- Surveillance techniques that monitor employees' behavior are being used with increasing frequency to control employee theft, as are undercover security personnel. While these techniques may be effective against shoplifters, employees can usually circumvent them. In addition, the financial costs of such strategies are huge, and employees generally resent electronic systems that monitor them.
- Keeping accurate records to limit the mishandling of funds or supplies. While this detects large cash shortages, it provides little deterrence to employee theft, and does not help in identifying the average employee who steals occasionally.
- Inspections (checking bags/lunch boxes). These are similar to "sting" operations that catch thieves in the act. However, the savings gained from the few people who get caught does not compensate for the negative environment that results from the mistrust of employees.

Both personnel selection and these control approaches assume that employees are greedy or morally lax; these strategies attempt to screen out potential thieves or limit opportunities to steal for any remaining dishonest employees in the workplace. Organizations using these approaches do not try to understand the nature of employee theft; they may assume employees steal for personal gain, without taking into consideration organizational factors that might contribute to theft.

Alternative approaches derive from the workplace theories of theft. First, it has previously been suggested that a positive climate throughout the workgroup would foster norms that discourage employee theft. Derived from the organizational climate and deterrence literature, this strategy is consistent with a top-down approach to theft prevention. The highly visible development, communication, and enforcement of company policies regarding employee theft can promote a strong anti-theft climate. Research on sexual harassment strongly supports this (Dekker & Barling, 1995). Consistent with social learning theory that emphasizes person X environment interactions, this research showed that company policies were most effective for employees most likely to engage in sexual harassment.

Consistent with organizational fairness theory, some specific recommendations to control theft would include improving relationships between employees and employers, reducing marginality (e.g., promote long-term employment), introducing employee ownership (shares in the company), and changing the way grievances are handled (Tucker, 1989). Other suggestions include treating employees with dignity, respect and trust (Greenberg, 1990, 1993), encouraging managers and supervisors to build non-adversarial relationships with employees, striving to enrich employees' jobs, providing opportunities for disgruntled employees to vent their emotions, and providing a model of organizational integrity (Taylor, 1986).

In keeping with payment equity theory, if adequate and fair compensation cannot be provided, employee theft can still be reduced by adequately explaining the basis for the inequity in an informative and interpersonally sensitive manner (Greenberg, 1990, 1993). A major benefit of these workplace interventions is that they are very inexpensive to implement.

CONCLUSION

The most important point to be emphasized is that none of the person-based or workplace-based theories/preventive strategies alone will effectively explain/reduce all instances of employee theft. The nature of employee theft is complex in that it results from an interaction of personal and organizational factors. Therefore, any comprehensive theory or preventive strategy should consider all of the different factors that contribute to employee theft. One last thought: Why do we continue to emphasize employee theft rather than the "flipside" which is employer exploitation? Changing our focus to include both employee theft and employer exploitation would simultaneously expand our research agenda and increase the likelihood that intervention would be more successful.

AUTHOR NOTES

Greenberg, Department of Psychology, and Barling, School of Business, Queen's University, Kingston, Ontario K7L 3N6.

Financial support from the Social Sciences and Humanities Research Council of Canada, the School of Business, and Imperial Oil to Julian Barling are gratefully acknowledged.

REFERENCES

Adams, J. S. (1965) Inequity in social exchange. In L. Berkowitz (Ed.), *Advances in Experimental Social Psychology* (vol. 2, pp. 267–299). San Diego, CA: Academic Press.

American Management Association (1977) *Crimes Against Business Project: Background, Findings, and Recommendations*. New York: American Management Association.

Astor, S. D. (1972) Who's doing the stealing? *Management Review*, **61**, 34–35.

Bacas, H. (1987) To stop a thief. *Nation's Business*, **75**, 16–23.

Bales, J. (1988) Integrity tests: Honest results? *APA Monitor*, **19**, 1, 4.

Bandura, A. (1977) *Social Learning Theory*. Englewood Cliffs, NJ: Prentice-Hall.

Barling, J. & Gallagher, D. (in press) Part-time employment. In C. L. Cooper and I. T. Robertson (Eds), *International Review of Industrial and Organizational Psychology* (vol. 11). Chichester, UK: Wiley.

Baumer, T. L. & Rosenbaum, D. P. (1984) *Combating Retail Theft: Programs and Strategies*. Boston, MA: Butterworth.

Black, D. (1987) The elementary forms of conflict management. Unpublished paper prepared for the distinguished Lecturer Series, School of Justice Studies, Arizona State University, Tempe, Arizona.

Bologna, J. (1980) Why employees steel—CPAs' and DPers' views. *Security Management*, **24**, 112–113.

Brown, T. S. & Pardue, J. (1985) Effectiveness of Personnel Selection Inventory in reducing drug store theft. *Psychological Reports*, **56**, 875–881.

Caudill, D. W. (1988) How to recognize and deter employee theft. *Personnel Administrator*, **33**, 86—90.

Clark, J. P. & Hollinger, R. C. (1981) *Theft by Employees in Work Organizations*. Minneapolis, MN: University of Minnesota, Department of Sociology.

Cressey, D. (1953) *Other People's Money: A Study in the social Psychology of Embezzlement*. Glencoe, IL: Free Press.

Dekker, I. & Barling, J. (1995) Personal and organizational predictors of self-reported sexual harassment in the workplace. Manuscript submitted for publication, School of Business, Queen's University, Kingston, Ontario K7L 3N6.

Employee Polygraph Protection Act of 1988. 29 U.S.C. Sec. 2001–2009.

Franklin, A. P. (1975) Internal theft in a retail organization: A case study. Unpublished PhD dissertation, The Ohio State University.

Gibbs, J. (1975) *Crime, Punishment and Deterrence*. New York: Elsevier.

Greenberg, J. (1990) Employee theft as a reaction to underpayment inequity: The hidden cost of pay cuts. *Journal of Applied Psychology*, **75**, 561–568.

Greenberg, J. (1993) Stealing in the name of justice: Informational and interpersonal moderators of theft reactions to underpayment inequity. *Organizational Behavior and Human Decision Processes*, **54**, 81–103.

Greenberg, L. & Barling, J. (1995) Predicting employee aggression: The roles of person behaviours and workplace factors. Manuscript in preparation, Department of Psychology, Queen's University, Kingston, Ontario K7L 3N6.

Guastello, S. J. & Rieke, M. L. (1991) A review and critique of honesty test research. *Behavioral Sciences and the Law*, **9**, 501–523.

Hartnett, J. J. (1990) A note on the PEOPLE survey: EEOC data and validation of the honesty scale. *Journal of Psychology*, **125**, 489–491.

Hawkins, R. (1984) Employee theft in the restaurant trade: Forms of ripping off by waiters at work. *Deviant Behavior*, **5**, 47–69.

Hollinger, R. C. (1986) Acts against the workplace: Social bonding and employee deviance. *Deviant Behavior*, **7**, 53–75.

Hollinger, R. C. & Clark, J. P. (1982) Employee deviance: A response to the perceived quality of the work experience. *Work and Occupations*, **9**, 97–114.

Hollinger, R.C. & Clark, J. P. (1983a) *Theft by Employees*. Lexington, MA: Lexington Books.

Hollinger, R. C. & Clark, J. P. (1983b) Deterrence in the workplace: Perceived certainty, perceived severity, and employee theft. *Social Forces,* **62,** 398–418.

Hollinger, R. C., Slora, K. B. & Terris, W. (1992) Deviance in the fast-food restaurant: Correlates of employee theft, altruism, and counterproductivity. *Deviant Behavior,* **13,** 155–184.

Johns, G. (1987) The great escape. *Psychology Today,* **21,** 30–33.

Jones, J. W., Joy, D. S., Werner, S. H. & Orban, J. A. (1991) Criterion-related validity of a preemployment integrity inventory: A large scale between-groups comparison. *Perceptual and Motor Skills,* **72,** 131–136.

Jones, J. W., Slora, K. B. & Boye, M. W. (1990) Theft reduction through personnel selection: A control group design in the supermarket industry. *Journal of Business and Psychology,* **5,** 275–279.

Jones, J. W. & Terris, W. (1984) *The Organizational Climate of Honesty: An Empirical Investigation.* Technical Report No. 27. Park Ridge, IL: London House Press.

Kamp, J. & Brooks, P. (1991) Perceived organizational climate and employee counterproductivity. *Journal of Business and Psychology,* **5,** 447–458.

Kantor, S. (1983) How to foil employee crime. *Nation's Business* (July), 38–39.

Lipman, M. (1978) *Stealing: How America's Employees are Stealing their Companies Blind.* New York: Harper's Magazine Press.

Lydon, K. (1984) Employee theft: A costly fringe benefit. *Security World* (April), 27–31.

Mars, G. (1974) Dock pilferage: A case study in occupational theft. In P. Rock & M. McIntosh (Eds), *Deviance and Control* (pp. 209–228). London: Tavistock Institute.

Mars, G. (1982) *Cheats at Work.* London: George Allen & Unwin.

McDaniel, M. A. & Jones, J. W. (1988) Predicting employee theft: A quantitative review of a standardized measure of dishonesty. *Journal of Business and Psychology,* **2,** 327–345.

McLean Parks, J. & Kidder, D. L. (1994) "Till death us do part . . .": Changing work relationships in the 1990s. In C. L. Cooper and D. M. Rousseau (Eds), *Trends in Organizational Behavior* (vol. 1, pp. 111–136). Chichester, UK: Wiley.

Merriam, D. (1977) Employee theft. *Criminal Justice Abstracts,* **9,** 380–386.

Merton, R. T. (1938) Social structure and anomie. *American Sociological Review,* **3,** 672–682.

Morgenstern, D. (1977) *Blue Collar Theft in Business and Industry.* Springfield, VA: National Technical Information Service.

Owens, W. A. (1976) Background data. In M. D. Dunnette (Ed.), *Handbook of Industrial and Organization Psychology.* Chicago: Rand McNally.

Palmiotto, M. J. (1983) Labor, government, and court reaction to detection of deception services in the private sector. *Journal of Security Administration,* **6,** 31–42.

Robin, G. D. (1969) Employees as offenders. *Journal of Research in Crime and Delinquency,* **6,** 17–33.

Slora, K. B. (1989) An empirical approach to determining employee deviance base rates. *Journal of Business and Psychology,* **4,** 199–219.

Taylor, R. R. (1986) The work environment: A positive guide to theft deterrence. *Personnel Journal,* **65,** 36–40.

Terris, W. (1982) Personnel selection as a method to reduce employee theft. *Journal of Security Administration,* **5,** 53–65.

Terris, W. & Jones, J. W. (1982) Psychological factors related to employee theft in the convenience store industry. *Psychological Reports,* **51,** 1219–1238.

Tittle, C. R. & Logan, C. H. (1973) Sanctions and deviance: Evidence and remaining questions. *Law and Society Review*, **7**, 371–392.

Tucker, J. (1989) Employee theft as social control. *Deviant Behavior*, **10**, 319–334.

Willis, R. (1986) White-collar crime: The threat from within. *Management Review*, **75**, 22–32.

CHAPTER 4

Service Quality

Benjamin Schneider and Beth Chung
University of Maryland, USA

Today the business world is changing radically. It's hardly a news
flash that we have entered an era of fierce competition—one in which
truly satisfying, even delighting, the customer is absolutely crucial
not only to business success but even to business survival.[1]

Much has been said and much has been written about quality and almost
of all of it has been with regard to the quality of products—automobiles,
refrigerators, portable telephones, and so forth. Yet, most of us engage in
and buy services on an almost daily basis, whereas we only purchase
products, especially the durables like those listed, occasionally. The
mechanic at the auto dealer, the service person who comes to repair the
refrigerator, and the repair person who takes care of our cellular phone;
these are service people. But in addition to the service people who care
for products (that is the *smallest* segment of the service world) there are
millions of people who deliver services that do not involve repair and, in
many cases, that involve no tangible product at all.

For example, a visit to the bank to cash a check is not accompanied by
an evaluation of the cash you receive but of the experience in getting the
cash; an airplane trip from New York to Washington is not evaluated on
whether you get there but what happens during the flight. Here is the
rule: the less tangible the product received in an encounter the more the
encounter is a service encounter.

And service business is *big* business:[2]

- Two-thirds (some would say more) of US GNP is accounted for by the
  service sector; the figure is slightly less in the EEC
- In the past three decades or so, the service economy in the US has

generated some 50 million new jobs and it is this service sector that
has softened each recession experienced in this time period
- As the baby-boomers age, the service economy will only continue to
  expand because the boomers will demand more and more services,
  especially healthcare services, as they age

In the present chapter, we introduce some ideas that have been found
to be useful in thinking about differences between services and products
and the implications of those differences for the management of service
quality.

SERVICE ATTRIBUTES

It has been only 25 years since marketers began thinking about ways in
which the marketing of services might differ from the marketing of
products. They began this journey into service quality when they
realized that services did not come in the neat little packages typical of
products. Fundamental questions in marketing concerning distribution
systems, packaging, delivery, and so forth took on new light when
confronting the kinds of intangibles that were becoming increasingly
dominant in the US and Western European economies. It became clear to
some marketing practitioners and academics, both in the US and in
Europe (particularly France and Scandinavia), that the intangibility of
many of the "products" being offered required some new ways of
thinking about precisely what is being marketed in the service sector.[3]
In the late 1970s and early 1980s there was much debate over the ways
in which services differed from products. Eventually the services
marketing community came to some agreement on three continua along
which services and products might be arrayed:

- Intangibility
- Simultaneous production and consumption
- Customer participation in production

It is important to note that these are continua, not dichotomies, since
most services have an accompanying product and most products have
accompanying services. However, the continua are useful at the
extremes, and we will speak primarily to the lessons learned at the
extremes.

Intangibility is the primary defining characteristic of a service; in the
extreme, a service maximally differs from a product due to its
intangibility. Services consist of experiences, acts, or processes rather

than objects that are verifiable in terms of size, weight, and space. The intangibility of services makes it difficult for service businesses to assess the performance of employees, and makes it difficult for customers to assess value; service quality is in the delivery experiences people have, and these are not easily verifiable for the business or for the customer.

Consider going to a symphony or the theatre. The service is in the delivery because there is no tangible present. Customers have their experiences, not a tangible product they can take with them, as the outcome. The size, weight, and space of the outcome, as with products, are irrelevant issues. And yet, the experience can be very powerful indeed.

Service businesses that adopt a product mentality, and most do, try to count or quantify how well they are doing *vis-à-vis* service quality. For example, bank tellers are evaluated on the number of transactions they complete, the accuracy of their cash drawer at the end of the day, and the number of times their phone rings prior to them picking it up. Warmth and courtesy in carrying out these activities in delivery to customers are not judged but these are the kinds of intangible features of service delivery on which customers evaluate service quality.

Simultaneous production and consumption (simultaneity) is a second continuum on which services and products may be arrayed. Simultaneity refers to the idea that services are typically produced and consumed in a single cycle as compared to products which can be produced at one time and place, then transferred to another place for inventory, and transferred yet again for sale—only to be followed by transport home for consumption. Services, on the other hand, basically have no shelf life.

For instance, airplane seats on the 5:00 p.m. flight on Airline X from JFK to LAX on 19 July 1995 will only exist once; the seat cannot be inventoried for use at a later point in time. Hotel beds in hotel rooms on particular nights only exist once. Beethoven's *Fifth* at the Philharmonic by the visiting Cleveland Orchestra on 20 May 1997 will only exist once. These services are produced and consumed simultaneously because, if not consumed when produced, they will never exist again. And services must be where they are needed—overbooked flights from JFK to LAX cannot be compensated for by extra seats on planes from DCA to ATL; similarly, hotel rooms needed in New Orleans cannot just be added to existing hotels in San Diego—the rooms must be where the need is. The point is that the simultaneity of services makes it difficult to forecast and adjust supply and demand; one cannot simply have the supplier courier over some extra planes.

Simultaneity presents unique problems for the management of service quality. Consider the fact that when a Chevrolet is produced the consumer is not there to watch production but he or she is there to watch production when the bank teller serves them; the airplane ride happens with you on the plane; the symphony is played with you listening to and watching production. The problem for service organizations is that production is visible, and is not buffered from the customer. This makes delivery (production) a key to the service quality equation. *How to manage delivery in ways that take into account the presence of the customer is a key challenge for service firms.*

Customer participation is a third continuum on which services differ from products. For many services, not only are customers *present* for production but they actually *participate* in production. Some services (e.g. medical services) depend upon the customer to provide the information that is the raw material to be transformed into the service outcome. Customers directly participate in the actual delivery of their own service in other ways as well. Examples include customer use of ATMs, customers bussing their own tables at fast food restaurants, customers choosing their own clothes off the rack in retail stores, customers making all of the arrangements for trips, vacations, tours, and so forth. In these ways, customers can be said to be "partial employees" or "coproducers" in the services they receive.

While simultaneity is a problem for service firms, having customers participate in production is really traumatic! How does a service firm recruit, select, socialize, train and otherwise motivate and guide a customer? If customers are not only customers but employees, too, should they be treated as if they are employees? Do customers fear losing their job? Are customers committed to the service firm? How can you reward customers to get them to behave as you want them to behave?

And yet, despite the problems they pose, customers participating in production of both products and services can be a valuable asset to a firm. Customer participation can yield insights not salient or available to regular employees. This is why product companies like 3M, Ford, and others have customer panels to whom they go for advice on everything from design, to marketing, to . . . service. This is how Xerox was able to avoid bankruptcy, why IBM fooled everyone and has been able to remake itself, and why local retailers like Hechinger's (a home products do-it-yourself retailer in the mid-Atlantic) have been able to compete successfully with national retailers (like Home Depot) who enter their marketplaces.

Simultaneity and customer participation are also reasons why companies are concerned with more than simply ensuring that transactions happen reliably. Companies like Ritz-Carlton are now working on establishing *relationships* with customers, relationships that transcend the transactional to create the levels of commitment and loyalty we associate with strong and valuable interpersonal relationships.[4]

In summary, these three attributes of service make the production of service quality a different, and perhaps more difficult, challenge than the production of product quality. In the production of products, periodic interventions are possible to assess quality prior to the time the end-user consumer uses the product. For service delivery, once the delivery process begins, it goes—planes do not turn back due to nasty cabin attendants and concerts do not begin anew when the trumpet player's embouchure collapses. Services unfold as wholes—for all to see. If all are there to see services unfold, and if service quality is in the delivery experience, then it follows that the conditions for delivery must be optimal for service quality to be achieved. In the next section we report on some research that suggests a complex bundle of conditions must be present for the customer to experience superior service quality.

CONDITIONS THAT PROMOTE THE SERVICE QUALITY EXPERIENCE[5]

With the whole world watching, control over the quality of service delivery lies in the situation created by the organization for the service deliverer. The tone or atmosphere that surrounds service delivery is the key to service quality. We call this tone or atmosphere the *climate for service quality*.

Research indicates that there are two critical sets of policies, practices and procedures that constitute a climate for service quality; when employees report these exist, *customers* report superior service quality:

- *Demonstrated concern for the customer*—soliciting *and using* customer feedback on service quality; staffing and training programs that emphasize service quality; logistical support (equipment and supplies) for service quality; an enthusiastic (flexible) not bureaucratic (rule-based) approach to service; and, a high-quality core service. The "core service" refers to the *raison d'être* of the business: food in a restaurant, medical treatment in a hospital, and the quality of the score itself at the symphony.
- *Demonstrated concern for the employees who deliver service*—considerate supervision; training and career development and planning programs; supportive socialization to the job; being proud of the organization and what it stands for; and, facilitating rather than inhibiting work effectiveness. The latter refers to such issues as keeping politics to a

minimum, and the dispensation of rewards based on merit rather than political connections.

When these two sets of conditions exist, employees are surrounded by cues and clues that service quality is not only appropriate but expected. The very conditions of the work and workplace breed an atmosphere in which the delivery of superior service quality is the norm; the situation promotes the message that service quality is valued. It is easy for employees in such conditions to believe that management truly believes in, that management truly values, superior service quality. Note that this belief on the part of employees is based on the conditions management creates in the workplace; the belief is *not* based on what management *says* it believes in.

One reason why the creation of a climate for service quality is important has to do with the intangibility of services. Because services lack external attributes that can themselves connote quality, services depend on the delivery experience for much of the determination of quality. Beethoven's *Fifth* and Shakespeare's *Macbeth* are wonderful accomplishments but they can be of very poor quality if delivered badly. The challenge is to have the core of the service, the music or the play, be excellent and have excellence in delivery, too. Having a climate for service quality surrounds the service deliverer with the quality imperative, an imperative that gets reflected in *customer* perceptions of service quality.

In one study, for example, both employees and customers of branch banks were asked to rate the quality of service of their branch—customers reported on the quality of service received and employees reported on the quality of service delivered.[6] Figure 4.1 shows the results of the answers to these ratings of service quality. In Figure 4.1 each dot represents a bank branch with the data from customers and employees plotted where they intersect. Overall there is a clear relationship between employee and customer reports on service quality at the branch; the relationship is not perfect but it is strong (the statistical correlation shown by the pattern of dots in Figure 4.1 is $r = 0.67$). These kinds of results have been replicated many times since the original study in 1980 and they reveal the importance of employees perceiving a service quality emphasis from within their own organization in order for the customers they serve to have a superior service quality experience.

A second reason why climate is important has to do with the joint issues of simultaneity and customer participation. Simultaneity requires that, once service delivery begins, it completely unfolds—there are no opportunities for quality control checks because production, delivery, and consumption occur essentially simultaneously. Thus, quality control

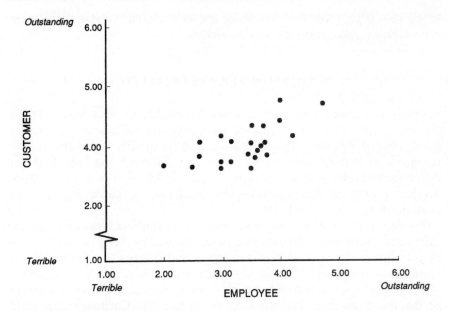

Figure 4.1 Relationship between employee and customer perceptions of service quality delivered (employees) and received (cuistomers)

exists only to the extent that the policies, practices, and procedures connoting a service climate exist. Similarly, customer participation requires that the climate exist so that appropriate *customer* behavior is reinforced and expected. Customers, like employees, need cues and clues to the behaviors expected and required of them. However, because they are customers, they cannot simply be ordered around; they must be surrounded by behavioral messages connoting for them what is required of them. The message is in the climate as portrayed to customers by employees. In other words, there is a chain of practices, policies and procedures that begins with management action, proceeds through employee perceptions of a climate for service quality to employee behavior, and it is employee behavior toward customers that culminates in customer perceptions of service quality.

Climate is not easy to manage because it is comprised of a package or bundle of policies, practices and procedures. There is no one magic bullet that makes it happen. Climate requires many activities in at least the two domains noted earlier for it to be perceived by employees and by customers. Just training, or just work facilitation, or just considerate supervision simply won't do; climate is in the package or bundle of activities all connoting and disseminating a common theme. And when employees report that such a climate for service quality exists, customers report they receive superior service quality.

IS QUALITY ALWAYS QUALITY?

Suppose you created a climate for service quality in your hotel. Would the same climate for service quality yield customer satisfaction at another hotel? One of the newer thoughts about service quality is that the quality required to satisfy customers differs for different markets and for different market segments. Service quality at Motel 6 is different from service quality at Ritz–Carlton—but both can be satisfying to their customers. How can this be?

The fact of the matter is that customers go to different types of hotels for different reasons and with different expectations. They may go to a Motel 6 on a business trip because it is convenient and inexpensive. At Motel 6, a clean, attractive room with a good shower may yield satisfaction because it meets or perhaps exceeds expectations—for a motel in the Motel 6 segment of the motel market. The same room at the Ritz–Carlton might yield dissatisfaction—people who go to the Ritz, even the same people who also go to Motel 6, expect different amenities and a different kind of relationship with the staff. They may go to a Ritz–Carlton to be spoiled and pampered, expecting staff to be unusually courteous and understanding, responsive, and especially attentive to their individual needs.

Our work tells us that for service businesses to have satisfied customers they must deliver the kind of service quality that meets and exceeds the expectations of the customers they want to keep. Motel 6 should not try to be Ritz–Carlton because they operate in a different segment of the hotel market. In a segment where tender loving care is the expectation (e.g., a Ritz–Carlton) then TLC must be delivered; where speed is the competitive strategy (e.g., a 7–11), then speed must be delivered; where attention to individual needs is the competitive strategy (e.g., a financial advisor), then individual attention must be provided. Understanding the segment of the market in which a firm competes is the key to the management of its climate for service quality.

The challenge for a service business is to derive a competitive market strategy, advertise to the desired market in ways that create a specific set of expectations, then manage the business to deliver against those expectations in ways that exceed the competition. The key to customer satisfaction in a service business is to deliver the quality that exceeds customer expectations *in that market segment*. Service businesses that understand this are able to create a climate for service quality required to exceed the expectations of the customers they want to keep.

They do this by emphasizing to everyone the market segment in which they want to compete through all of their management practices—from human resources to marketing and from facilities to finance. This is necessary because the climate for service quality depends on many activities and it is the way these activities are carried out that connotes for employees and customers the *kind* of quality (not the *level* of quality) that is required. These activities or policies, practices, and procedures give employees cues as to the kinds of behaviors that are expected, rewarded, and recognized. They will then have an implicit contract with the employer to deliver on those behaviors. Different market segments will, in essence, communicate different sets of behaviors that are needed from employees.

At Ritz–Carlton, staffing and training practices emphasize care and concern; marketing promotes the TLC image; finance is less concerned with cost-cutting and efficiency and more concerned with quality; and facilities management is given the go-ahead to produce a physically attractive and sumptuous "feel". At Motel 6 this just won't work, either for the bottom line or for the customer.

Table 4.1 shows a useful, though somewhat oversimplified, way of thinking about these strategic marketing issues for the delivery of service quality. Table 4.1 presents three issues along which service firm strategy can be conceptualized: speed, tender loving care, and customization:

- *Speed* refers to being responsive, prompt, reliable, and quick

Table 4.1 Market segment typology

Service segment	Speed	TLC[a]	Customization
Adequate service	0	0	0
Responsive service	+	0	0
Friendly service	0	+	0
Tailored service	0	0	+
Good service	+	+	0
Cold service	+	0	+
Caring service	0	+	+
Terrific service	+	+	+

[a] Denotes Tender Loving Care.

Note: Price is the wild card. There are no minus signs ("−") in the table due to the assumption that negative expectations for speed, TLC and/or customization is not a meaningful concept since such expectations would likely yield an absence of customers.

Source: Adapted from Schneider, B. (1994) HRM—A service prospective: Towards a customer-focused HRM. *International Journal of Service Industry Management*, **5**, 64–76.

- *TLC* refers to staff behaviors like courtesy, understanding, empathy, interpersonal warmth, friendliness, and consideration
- *Customization* in the service refers to the extent to which service is tailored to each individual customer versus being mass produced and generically delivered

All facets of the business must be in line with regard to the strategic market segment in which the business competes.[7]

Any particular organization can decide to be average or excellent on any one or all of these service factors. As Table 4.1 shows, zeros (0) indicate average performance on a factor while pluses (+) indicate excellent performance on a factor. Combining these three factors and mapping out all possible combinations of zeros and pluses, there are eight potential market segments. Furthermore, we suggest that customers make various trade-offs between these facets of a service and price, substituting price for one or more of the three service delivery facets. For example, we identify Motel 6 as an "adequate service" which, being adequate on all three, chooses to compete on price—while attempting to exceed the competition in terms of the quality issues. We identify Ritz–Carlton as being a "terrific" service which is high on all three facets so they compete less on price and more on quality. Motel 6 and Ritz–Carlton operate in different segments of the hotel industry and their customers come with different sets of expectations regarding speed, TLC, customization—and price too. The critical issues for both are the following:

- Regardless of the market in which it competes, the firm must be clear about its market segment.
- Once clarity about market segment is achieved, all facets of management must be aligned against that market segment, the goal being to exceed the competition in service quality in that segment. This is accomplished by creating a climate for service quality appropriate for the market segment.

We continuously emphasize, as is obvious by now, the importance of competing in a market segment. This is because service quality is not an absolute; there is not good service quality and bad service quality, there is superior service quality relative to the competition in the chosen market segment. In other words, a business can "over-service" in the sense that, for example, competing in a segment where speed is critical, the business emphasizes TLC. Service quality is relative and the important relative in service quality is the competition in the market segment. And, service quality that is superior to the competition yields long-term profits for the organization.

To close this section of the chapter, we reflected on our own experiences with hotels and the ways in which a set of expectations was exceeded and remembered—in particular, the Blue Earth Super 8 Motel in Blue Earth, North Dakota. What can a Super 8 Motel do to distinguish itself from the competition? We reproduce here the description of the philosophy and attributes of the owners of the Blue Earth Super 8. One of us can personally vouch for the accuracy of the description provided of their motel by Mickey and Ernie Wingen—and for the clear edge it has on its competition!

BLUE EARTH SUPER 8 PHILOSOPHY
Friendliness, a pleasant atmosphere, comfort and relaxation, a variety of services at Budget Prices—all this is the aim of your hosts, Mickey and Ernie Wingen, here in the Blue Earth Super 8 Motel.
The Early American decor is designed to assist you in being comfortable and at ease. Your hosts have spent thousands of hours handcrafting each decoration and each piece of furniture. For your added pleasure, there is the hot tub and the exercise room, the lounge and fireplace, the landscaped court, and the continental breakfast with homemade rolls. You will find an air of friendly hospitality, and our motel personnel all wish to meet your needs as closely as possible.
In return, we ask that you show your appreciation by helping us keep the building and grounds neat, and to treat the fixtures in an acceptable manner.

FUTURE TRENDS IN SERVICE QUALITY

People interested in service quality have moved from attempting to understand differences between services and products, to attempting to understand the conditions that must exist to deliver superior service quality, to understanding the relative nature of service quality and the use of service quality as a competitive advantage in the market place. There is still much to be learned both about the customers to whom service is delivered and the firms that deliver service quality to those customers.

Future Customer Research and Practice: Customer Needs

There has been considerable interest, obviously, in the assessment of customer satisfaction and customer perceptions of service quality. The basic model for most of this work has been the idea that customer perceptions of service encounters are framed by them in terms of their expectations; the difference between expectations and perceptions is satisfaction. Hence, our incessant emphasis on exceeding customer expectations in a market segment, that is, exceeding the competition in delivering service quality.

One emerging area of interest in customer satisfaction moves away from the concept of customer expectations to the concept of customer needs—especially quite basic needs like the needs for security, esteem, and justice.[8] Needs are different from expectations in that expectations are conscious, specific, short-term, and at a surface level while needs are unconscious until activated, more global, deep, and long-term. We may react to violations of expectations with disappointment or dissatisfaction; we react to violations of basic needs with anger or even outrage. Dissatisfy a customer and they will be unhappy; violate a customer's needs and you will lose them. This is analogous to the difference between competencies that help a manager succeed (career potential) and those elements that lead a manager to fail (career jeopardy). Like managerial competency dimensions, expectations and needs are on two different dimensions versus being ends on the same continuum.

Consider the need for esteem—the need to have one's self-esteem maintained and enhanced. By esteem, we mean a person's self-identity or self-concept, especially maintenance of a positive self-concept. Because service encounters are often face-to-face interpersonal interactions, customers' egos are on the line and there are many opportunities to violate the need for esteem.

Esteem needs can be violated in a number of ways. One way is by failing to understand and acknowledge the reality of a customer's dissatisfaction. In this case, the phrase "the customer is always right" rings true because what a customer *feels* is his or her reality and one cannot argue with such reality.

One of us once went to a New York hotel and discovered that her reservations were inexplicably cancelled and that she did not have a room. Instead of apologizing for any part in the mistake that may have been due to the hotel and proactively making other arrangements for her, the hotel personnel proceeded to explain what she must have done wrong. This was further compounded by having her wait 15 minutes before talking to a supervisor and 40 minutes before securing other facilities. As a customer (even a potential customer in this case), she felt belittled, disrespected, and dismissed. By not recognizing and appealing to the customer's esteem needs, the hotel risked losing a long-standing corporate account.

Information technology is another area in which customer needs for self esteem can easily be violated. We are very concerned that, in an attempt to reduce personnel costs, service businesses are doing everything possible to eliminate face-to-face contact between themselves and their customers through the introduction of information technology. This is dangerous for several reasons:

- Many people have technology phobias and are afraid to actually use technology because they fear they will look stupid to themselves and/or to the public. For example, we hypothesize that most people who do not use ATMs fail to do so because of threats to their esteem; they do not know how to use them and want to avoid looking stupid if they fail.
- When people are upset they want to have another person to whom they can express these feelings; encountering technology will simply exacerbate the problem. Voice-mail menus are already the bane of many people's daily lives; when it is an emergency, encountering a voice-mail menu will implicitly devalue the emergency, thus implicitly devaluing the caller.

In brief, the implications of information technology for the psychology of the customer and the degree to which the business can avoid violating basic customer needs is not well understood either by researchers or service firms. We hypothesize that, in their zeal to cut costs through technology, service businesses may be alienating their customers. This can be particularly dangerous at a time when the relationship between customer and firm is becoming a potential competitive advantage.

We could list hundreds of ways in which businesses unwittingly violate customer needs for esteem. Instead we will list a rule:

- Customers' esteem is most often violated when they publicly, or privately, feel disrespected, belittled or dismissed.

Future Research and Practice on Relationship Marketing[9]

Another emerging topic in the services literature is the concept of relationship marketing. Service firms are coming to realize that a focus on each transaction with a customer as an isolated event is not the way to build a relationship; it is the history of the transactions between customer and firm that makes for a relationship. Thus, in interpersonal relationships, when we interact a second and a third time, we behave differently than we did the first time; how can a firm establish a relationship with a customer if it behaves towards a customer the second and third time as if it were the first time each time? Service firms need to recognize that some kind of a relationship, in fact, does exist by the second and third encounter and that it is up to the organization to decide how to manage this relationship. This is the relationship management challenge. And, because service is so intangible and involves customers at least as observers and potentially also as coproducers, the challenge is very great indeed.

Precisely how to show customers that they are valued as well as desired is not presently very well understood. But it seems clear to us that a first level of attention would be to focus on issues concerned with service quality like those mentioned earlier: exceeding expectations *vis-à-vis* the competition and addressing customer needs in ways that enhance rather than violate needs for security, esteem and fairness. All of these require attention to many facets of the service relationship from the design of facilities to the role of technology, and from the nature of interpersonal relationships to the ways in which encountered problems are resolved.

Actually, technology can play an important role in establishing a relationship orientation compared to a transactional perspective with customers. For example, when we go to the bank to cash a cheque, why does the bank want to see our driver's license and copy down the license number every time we go? Why not put the driver's license number in the computer and let the teller just look at the picture for identification? In other words, why is it more difficult to get a cheque cashed by a teller than it is to get cash from the ATM? Why when doing a transaction at the ATM do you get a printed account balance update but when making a deposit with a teller you get no printed balance? Perhaps banks are telling us something: you get better service from ATMs than from tellers so use the ATM? That's a heck of a way to establish a relationship!

Hotel and airline reservations could similarly "remember" preferences and history, as could credit card companies. History is very important to building relationships and service firms must figure out how to acknowledge, reinforce, and demonstrate the value of history in dealing with their customers. As just one other example, consider the auto insurance policy holder who has had his policy with the company for 25 years and never had an accident or a speeding ticket. He gets into an accident while speeding and the next thing the company does is either (a) tries to cancel the policy, or (b) increases the premium by an astronomical amount. This is not the way to take history into account and honor a relationship!

SUMMARY AND CONCLUSION

In a brief number of pages we have tried to summarize some of the thinking and research being done with regard to service quality. We have focused on several fundamental issues with regard to service quality:

- *The nature of services*—their relative intangibility, simultaneity and the presence of the customer for service production, and the customer as coproducer.

- *The implications of the nature of service for the management of service businesses*—here we emphasized the necessity to create a climate for service quality in which all facets of the business "speak" through policies, practices and procedures, and the importance of exceeding the competition in service quality. We summarized research showing that when employees perceive their business as one that cares for service quality and cares for employee quality of worklife, *customers* report receiving superior service quality.
- *Strategic service quality management*—the ways in which service quality issues get played out in different market segments and the importance of strategic marketing for the management of the business. Here we emphasized the point that service quality is not an absolute but is relative to competition. The importance here, too, of alignment of the various facets of management to the strategic market segment was emphasized.
- *Emergent trends*—finally, two emergent trends in service quality, a focus on customer needs and a focus on firm–customer relationships, were discussed. A central issue in both cases became information technology. On the one hand, we presented the idea that an over-emphasis on information technology might defeat the ability of firms to deal effectively with customers' basic psychological needs. On the other hand, we noted the potential for such technology to assist in establishing a deeper psychological relationship with customers in the future by focusing on the history of the relationship.

The field of marketing has clearly dominated the issues addressed here although there has been some work by people interested in operations management and some by people interested in organizational behavior. Continued work in the organizational behavior field on the topic of services management is still very much needed, given the research that demonstrates the strong ties between what customers experience in the way of service quality and the kinds of experiences employees have in organizations. In order to truly understand customer behavior and customers' views of service quality, we must continue to try to understand employee experiences and behavior and how management practices affect these experiences and behaviors.

The topics of study in organizational behavior, from motivation to leadership and from job satisfaction to the study of organizational citizenship behaviors, take on new meaning when we demonstrate how internal functioning relates to the external consumer. Thus, in the past we have been concerned with understanding *internal* effects—productivity, absenteeism, turnover—of organizational behavior issues. Now we understand that these same behaviors and experiences can have implications for the *customers* of organizations, too. The unique competencies we bring to understanding service quality provide an exciting opportunity for those of us interested in these issues—and for the effective manager to take increasing control, through their management practices, of the service quality experiences their customers have.

ACKNOWLEDGMENT

We greatly appreciate the comments of Susan Schoenberger on an earlier version of this chapter.

REFERENCE NOTES

1. The quote comes from Richard C. Whiteley (1991) *The Customer Driven Company: Moving From Talk to Action.* Reading, MA: Addison-Wesley, p. 2.
2. See Gronroos, C. (1990) *Service Management and Marketing: Managing the Moments of Truth in Service Competition.* Lexington, MA: Lexington Books; Albrecht, K. & Zemke, R. (1985) *Service America: Doing Business in the New Service Economy.* New York: Dow Jones–Irwin.
3. Some important references to the history of service marketing and management can be found in the following sources: Lovelock, C. H. (1992) *Managing Services: Marketing, Operations, and Human Resources,* 2nd edn. Englewood Cliffs, NJ: Prentice-Hall; Bateson, J. E. G. (1992) *Managing Services Marketing,* 2nd edn. Fort Worth, TX: Dryden.
4. An introduction to what has come to be called "relationship marketing" can be found in Christopher, M., Payne, A. & Ballantyne, D. (1991) *Relationship Marketing: Bringing Quality Customer Service and Marketing Together.* London: Butterworth–Heinemann.
5. The research summarized in what follows here can be found in more detail in Schneider, B. & Bowen, D. E. (1995) *Winning the Service Game.* Boston, MA: Harvard Business School Press.
6. See Schneider, B. (1980) The service organization: Climate is crucial. *Organizational Dynamics,* Autumn, **9**, 52–65.
7. See the Schneider and Bowen (1995) citation at Note 5 above.
8. See the Schneider and Bowen (1995) citation at Note 5 above.
9. See Berry, L. L. (1995) *On Great Service.* New York: Free Press.

CHAPTER 5

Computer-Aided Systems for Organizational Learning

Paul S. Goodman
Carnegie Mellon University, Pittsburgh, USA

and

Eric D. Darr
University of California at Los Angeles, USA

Developing, using and maintaining knowledge is critical to compete in today's business climate (Day, 1994; Senge, 1990; Stata, 1989). Global business leaders such as Xerox, Merck, Shell Oil and Arthur Andersen S. C. recognize this need, and are building learning organizations as part of their central strategy for achieving performance excellence.

But, creating a learning organization is a challenge. For example, large diversified firms must transfer knowledge across different divisions to be successful at organizational learning. Geographic distance, differences in experience, differences in rewards, and differences in attitudes inhibit knowledge transfer across organizational divisions (Cohen & Levinthal, 1990; Darr, 1994). Multinational organizations face an even greater challenge (Keller & Chinta, 1990). Managers in global firms face the difficult task of getting employees to effectively collaborate and share expertise unbounded by language, culture, space and/or time. How can organizations facilitate both local creativity and global knowledge diffusion?

This paper examines how new technology in the form of computer-aided learning systems (CALS) facilitates the exchange of knowledge across distributed organizational units. We focus on the role of technology as a transmitter because despite its potential, it is a relatively unexplored area of organizational learning. Computer-aided systems are

Trends in Organizational Behavior, Volume 3. Edited by C. L. Cooper and D. M. Rousseau
© 1996 John Wiley & Sons Ltd

changing organizational processes such as communication (Kiesler & Sproull, 1987), group decision making (Kiesler, Siegel & McGuire, 1984), coordination (Rice & Shook, 1990), and collaborative work (Kraut, Galegher, Fish & Chalfonte, 1992). Yet, only a few studies deal with computer-aided systems for facilitating organizational learning with a firm (Sproull & Kiesler, 1986; Orlikowski, 1993; Constant, Sproull & Kiesler, 1995; Goodman & Darr, 1995). This chapter charts out research opportunities in this area.

We begin this exploration by first clarifying some basic concepts and then identifying some lessons from the existing literature. We follow by specifying some research trends and opportunities.

BASIC CONCEPTS

Organizational learning is a complex concept. Several authors have offered views about the steps and outcomes associated with organizational learning (Argyris & Schon, 1978; Levitt & March, 1988; Huber, 1991; Nonaka, 1994). A theme common across the various definitions is that learning can be derived from one's own experiences or the experiences of others. We focus on learning from others in a setting where there are geographically distributed units performing some similar functions. Learning at one level occurs when one unit discovers a problem, seeks a solution from another unit, the other unit contributed a solution which is then adopted by the first unit. Adopting and contributing are necessary, but not sufficient, for organizational learning.

The distinction between organizational and individual level learning can further delineate our understanding of organizational learning (Argote, 1993; Kim, 1993). Consider the following examples. A marketing manager in Los Angeles has a problem with the sales of a new product, and seeks help from the company's marketing manager in London. Let's also assume the London manager contributes a solution which is adopted and implemented successfully in Los Angeles. At this point, the exchanges of problems and solutions are at the *individual level*. To create organizational level learning:

- The problem–solution exchanges and consequences need to be *communicated* and known by other organizational members
- There needs to be some form of organizational *memory* which stores problem–solution exchanges and consequences (Walsh & Ungson, 1991; Walsh, 1995)
- There needs to be a way for organizational members to form *shared interpretations* about the new problem–solution exchanges and then

update organizational memory with their experiences (Brown & Duguid, 1991)

Computer-aided systems have some unique features for facilitating organizational learning. First, they can provide fast efficient communication, bridging space and time. Second, many systems have the capability of creating a stored history of problem–solution exchange experiences for all members. Third, computer-aided systems provide a mechanism where multiple members dynamically share solutions and update their problem–solution experiences.

The following example illustrates these three features. A leading international airline has constructed a CALS which greatly improves its scheduling process. The scheduling process concerns decisions about which airplane to use on a given route, or what number of gates to occupy at a given airport. It requires input from 13 separate functional groups, which are geographically distant from each other. Using paper memos and fax technology, the scheduling process often took weeks and missed valuable input from one or more groups. The decision-making time was reduced, while the decision quality was improved by linking the groups together with a WAN (wide-area network), and developing a Lotus Notes process application (LAN). Current decisions are made through a series of discussion databases that allow all groups to simultaneously monitor and add to the process. Each new piece of knowledge is automatically copied to everyone's individual database regardless of the source. Past decisions can be viewed through a knowledge database which contains formatted records of previous issues and their resolutions. Through the CALS, the 13 groups are better able to share current knowledge and to access past experience.

Another example comes from an international consulting firm which developed a CALS to improve client satisfaction. For years, consultants had to rely on their personal network of contacts to meet client requests for information and/or help which fell outside their own individual realm of expertise. The sources for new information were limited by the size of a consultant's personal network. By electronically linking every consultant together with LANs and WANs, while developing knowledge databases containing previous consulting experience, industry information, and expert contacts, the number of sources for new information available to any single consultant was greatly increased. Additionally, discussion databases organized around specific topics allowed ongoing knowledge sharing between geographically distant consultants. Anyone at anytime in any location could monitor ongoing discussions, take away new insights, or join in, and add new knowledge through the CALS.

These two examples illustrate three defining characteristics of CALS, and how CALS are different from traditional e-mail systems:

- CALS allow knowledge sharing from many individuals to many other individuals. E-mail systems, using bulletin-boards, allow sharing from only one to many.
- CALS allow automatic knowledge storage and retrieval. E-mail systems do not automatically create memories.
- CALS allow development of shared interpretations by distributing recent knowledge changes to all individuals. E-mail systems have no such capability.

EXISTING RESEARCH

Several researchers have begun exploring CALS. Orlikowski (1993) investigated a CALS which allowed users to browse through previous experience which was stored in a collection of knowledge databases. The CALS also allowed for ongoing discussions between many individuals. Orlikowski (1993) found that although the system was designed for collaborative work, the existing incentive system and culture motivated individuals to use the CALS for their own personal gain.

Constant, Sproull and Kiesler (1995) investigated a CALS which allowed users to access technical expertise held by a community of practitioners. The answers to ongoing technical queries wee placed in a database which other users could access. Constant and colleagues found that the frequency of system use was relatively low, and that organizational citizenship factors influenced system use.

Finholt (1993) investigated a CALS which allowed users to ask for solutions to existing problems. The solutions were maintained in a knowledge database which other users could access. Finholt (1993) found that reward and culture factors generated relatively low system use.

Goodman and Darr (1995) investigated a CALS which allowed users to contribute and access knowledge labeled as "best practices". Anyone could submit a "best practice", and it could be about technical issues, sales or administration. Contributions to the system had to be approved by a central staff committee before appearing in the system. Goodman and Darr (1995), too, found relatively low system use, this time determined by the characteristics of problems and solutions that were to be exchanged, motivational issues, and the use of alternative transfer mechanisms.

CALS research suggests the following basic conclusions. Individuals are not always motivated to use CALS. There are costs (e.g. search time) associated with individual adoption from and contribution to CALS. Individuals adopting knowledge from a CALS must also have sufficient computer skills to access the system. They must be able to represent their problem in a way that others can contribute the viable solutions. Additionally, adopting knowledge from a CALS may alert others to an individual's weakness or need. There are inhibitors to contributing. Knowledge is seen as power, and knowledge sharing is perceived to weaken one's personal power. Also, there is little reward or recognition for contributions. Job pressures may not allow time to contribute. Contribution often occurs in an environment with few personal ties and no reciprocation.

While there are strong inhibitors to exchanging in a weak tie environment, there are also positive motivators. Constant, Sproull and Kiesler (1995) found that citizenship norms and individual technical competence facilitate adoption and contribution activities. One challenge in future research is to explore in more depth the motivational dilemmas to problem and solution exchange.

Whether there is a "learning" culture (i.e. norms and values that support adoption and contribution activities) will affect the use of CALS (Orlikowski, 1992). Research is needed to disentangle the effects of culture from other motivational inhibitors on CALS usage. We have argued that there are inherent inhibitors to adopting ideas and solutions from other geographically distributed units. One interesting question is to determine the process by which different forms of learning culture mitigate the effect of these inhibitors. For example, suppose that employees in a Los Angeles office adopt numerous solutions from other international offices, while employees in a New York office do not adopt solutions from other offices. We need to understand how the learning cultures (vs motivational factors) in the Los Angeles and New York offices contribute to the differential adoption rates.

The forms of the objects to be exchanged will affect CALS usage. Some existing research has focused on exchanging solutions to technical problems (Constant, Sproull & Kiesler, 1959). Other research (Goodman & Darr, 1995) which examined a more heterogeneous problem environment indicates that problem complexity and tacitness in problems and solutions inhibit exchanges using CALS. There is some indication that targeting CALS to more homogeneous environments improves rates of exchanges.

Computer-aided learning systems may complement or compete with the many formal and informal systems for exchanging knowledge across units which exist. For example, Goodman and Darr (1995) found that employees of a large service organization shared knowledge through 17 different transfer mechanisms. They also found informal "learning communities" where multiple electronic and non-electronic mechanisms were used in a complementary fashion for transferring problems and solutions. Understanding when alternative mechanisms will compete or complement CALS is a challenge for future research.

Finally, measuring system effectiveness is difficult. So few studies of CALS have been completed that it is difficult to define average system usage rates. Beyond usage, it is unclear what should be used as measures of system performance. For example, given that one purpose of CALS is to store knowledge for future use, what is the appropriate time frame for measuring effectiveness? One could measure the number or rate of knowledge adoptions. But this ignores the impact or use of the knowledge. It seems likely that CALS performance should be judged using multiple measures taken at different points in time. Also, the linkage between the effectiveness of specific exchanges and organizational effectiveness is not well understood.

The existing empirical research on CALS has provided some important insights on the learning process. We have tried to identify some selected findings and some new research challenges. In the next section, we offer some different research frames for thinking about the role of technology in the organizational learning process.

NEW RESEARCH FRAMES

By changing the assumptions underlying most current research concerning computer-aided learning systems, we create new research frames. The new research frames create new research opportunities.

Proactive vs Reactive

Many of the current studies focus on a reactive problem–solution exchange. A problem is identified in one setting. A CALS is then used to explore whether other units have experienced the same problem, and whether acceptable solutions have been identified. Alternative solutions are evaluated. Eventually, a solution is adopted and implemented.

The motivation to adopt knowledge would likely be higher in situations where users are facing an existing problem. Users may accept costs associated with learning and using a CALS if they believe that the system will help solve a problem. It also seems likely that the scope and importance of the problem for the user will determine individual motivation for system use. Generally, our understanding of knowledge adoption costs may not be complete if we only research users in reactive modes.

We suggest that research be done on CALS that are being used for proactive reasons. It is important to understand user motivation for using CALS to engage in playful searches. Under what conditions do users accept adoption costs even when there are no clear benefits? Playful searches for knowledge are important activities in a learning organization (Senge, 1990). A better understanding of users in proactive modes should help organizations realize learning benefits.

In addition to motivational issues about playful searches, we need to explore the method for search. In reactive scenarios, a person may broadcast a problem to other organizational members (Constant, Sproull & Kiesler, 1995), or search a library for solutions (Goodman & Darr, 1995). In playful searches, the area of exploration is likely to be broad.

Several iterative searches may be used to solicit knowledge from diffuse audiences. The interesting challenge is to understand more about how playful searches are undertaken. How long do they last? What heuristics are used? How do the searches vary by problem area or individual?

In our definition of organization learning the existence of a memory available to all organization members was a key criteria. In the reactive problem–solution matching scenario, the memory contains specific solutions keyed to problem areas. Playful search seems more about gathering new ideas, concepts or frames to think about organizational activities and processes. One question concerns how information would be represented in memory. Perhaps text-only representations would be insufficient to facilitate knowledge integration and adaptation. Image animation and other forms may be necessary to motivate and to assist playful search. Another question concerns how to access information in memory. For example, if a service employee has a technical problem with a machine, a search or indexing system that lets the person match the machine and its problem with information in memory is necessary. Alternatively, if the person wanted to engage in playful search about all machines, perhaps "matching systems" are not appropriate. Rather, a mechanism such as Lychos (Internet Web Crawler) is a better system. It allows more playful, broader searches. How can playful heuristics be designed? Or, should they be developed at all by others? If playfulness is idiographic to the user, the opportunity to develop individual heuristics may be sufficient.

Adopter-Contributor vs the Expert

Explicit in most CALS studies is the assumption that the organization is populated with problems and solutions, and the task is to facilitate matches. An alternative perspective is that problem–solution matches are very difficult, and the task is to match problems and experts. This perspective assumes that there is a class of problems and solutions where matches are very unlikely. This class includes: (a) problem statements which are difficult to specify; (b) problems with many possible solutions; (c) solutions which are difficult to articulate or roles to implement that are not well understood; and (d) problem and solution matches where results are not well known.

One of the research opportunities is understanding when problem–solution matches versus problem–expert matches would facilitate organizational learning. The specification of problem–solution characteristics above represents a first step in delineating when it may be more appropriate to use problem–expert matches.

Another issue is understanding more about the role of the expert. Even in the current research on problem–solution matches, the contributor often provides referrals to solving the problem rather than a specific solution (Constant, Sproull & Kiesler, 1995). Is the role of the expert to help clarify problem statements, refer to other experts, train the potential adopter, and so on? Understanding in a deep way what experts do seems to be an important next step in understanding problem–expert matches. Although our focus is on experts in a computer-aided learning environment, there are lots of expert-like examples in organizations today. For example, many companies have 800 numbers to solve internal or external technical problems. How do these technical assistance arrangements work in terms of what people do (i.e., the transactions and the effectiveness of these transactions)?

A related issue concerns the organizational arrangements for the expert. For example, there is a midwestern manufacturing corporation that has designated experts in specific areas. These experts, typically individual contributors, can be approached to solve problems in their areas. The requester has to pay for their services and share any benefits (e.g., cost savings) with the expert. That is, there is a free arrangement for billing the expert's time. Then, if the solutions are successful, the expert receives a percentage of the cost savings or new revenue. The basic point is that creating problem–expert matches with CALS requires understanding more about the role of the expert and the organizational infrastructure.

Intra-organizational vs Inter-organizational Relationships

Most current studies focus on learning across distributed units in the same organization. For example, Goodman and Darr (1995) studied a company that had 70 units, all doing the same activity, sales and service.

The research challenge is to examine learning across different organizations. The problem–solution exchanges could be with customers, suppliers, creditors and/or debtors. In these situations, the firms involved in the exchanges are likely concerned with different challenges or goals. Alternatively, exchanges could occur between firms sharing common challenges or goals, such as members of a research consortium or Japanese Kieretsu.

We have argued that using CALS for knowledge exchanges in the same organization is inherently very difficult. Attempting exchanges across organizations is even more difficult. Not only do different organizations pursue unique challenges and goals, but they use different languages to specify problems, have different problem distributions, and have different behavioral norms and attitudes. Additionally, members of different firms have fewer opportunities to develop strong ties. Most likely, problem–solution exchanges between different firms would take place in a weak tie environment. The exchange of knowledge is very difficult when no personal relationships, common cultures or shared superordinate goals are operating.

Despite the challenge, there are growing numbers of joint ventures, strategic alliances and consortiums. These organizational forms require inter-organizational cooperation and knowledge exchange to be successful. As more work is done in traditional multifirm organizations, as well as newer "virtual organizations", it will be important to understand the role of CALS in knowledge sharing between different firms. Additionally, current interest in the Internet as a potential CALS suggests that we should think about new ways of designing knowledge exchanges across different organizations.

The form of the relationship between organizations may act to reinforce or lessen the effects of the knowledge exchange barriers noted above. Inter-organizational relationships may be classified along a continuum which ranges from purely economic to purely relational. The relationship between a one-time buyer and seller would be an economic example. In this case, the only reason for a relationship is to transfer goods or services for money. The relationship between long-time suppliers and users would be a relational example. In this situation, the relationship may be based on trust and mutual need that has developed over time. Relational inter-organization arrangements have their roots in multiple interactions over a period of time. They also involve organizations that add value to each other, beyond simple economic gain.

The expectation is that the exchange of knowledge between organizations with a relational association may be easier than between economically linked organizations. Because relational inter-organizational relationships are built over time, there are multiple opportunities for the unique cultures, reward systems and practices of each firm to become known to the partner. Additionally, relationally linked organizations have developed some level of trust with each other. The added familiarity and trust associated with relational associations suggests that knowledge exchanges would be easier. The general idea is that attention should be given to the form of the inter-organizational relationship when researching the use of CALS for knowledge exchange.

The opportunities present for inter-organizational knowledge exchange may also act to reinforce or lessen the effects of the exchange barriers previously noted. Miner and Haunschild (1995) suggest that the opportunities for inter-organizational exchange will be partially determined by the frequency of experiences at the population level. For example, in the ocean-liner building business there is a relatively low frequency of product completion. There are many, many more houses or cars built in any given time period. The frequency of experience in the ocean-liner business is low. Miner and Haunschild (1995) suggest that inter-organizational knowledge exchanges will be more likely under conditions of low experience frequency, because no single firm will have sufficient experience to improve. Under conditions of low experience frequency, organizations may be more aggressive in searching for and acquiring external knowledge.

Opportunities for inter-organizational knowledge exchange may also be determined by the level of third-party intervention. For example, an active trade association may link organizations together in new ways. A trade association may become the mechanism for knowledge exchange. Alternatively, active intervention by government agencies may link organizations together in new ways. For example, the proposal process and the coordination activities conducted by the US Department of Defense created opportunities for knowledge exchange between multiple aerospace contractors. The general idea is that low frequencies of population level experiences and/or third-party interventions affect the opportunities for inter-organizational knowledge exchange. A greater number of exchange opportunities may offset some of the barriers to knowledge sharing.

Domestic vs International Exchanges

The current work on CALS has not only focused on knowledge exchanges within a single organization, but the research is limited to exchanges within the US. Knowledge exchange using CALS between geographically distributed units in one country is difficult. However, differences in cultures, languages, views about work, as well as markets make international knowledge exchange even more challenging. Yet, the potential importance and need of international knowledge transfer is growing. The research challenge is to understand the unique difficulties associated with international knowledge exchange.

While it is clear that knowledge exchanges in a cross-cultural context are difficult, several factors affect the probability of exchanging problems and solutions. First, the type of problem (i.e., the knowledge characteristics) may reinforce or reduce the effect of culture on international exchanges. The perception and understanding of certain classes of problems may be unaffected by cultural influences. For example, problems with machines or manufacturing processes that are common throughout the world would likely be unaffected. A problem with the stapler in a Xerox 5095 copier would seem to be very similar regardless of the machine location. The perception and understanding of other classes of problems may be greatly affected by cultural influences. For example, problems which overlap with strongly held national norms or values would likely be affected. The perceptions of problems dealing with hierarchies or employee empowerment would likely vary across nations due to differences in beliefs about power and distance (Hofstede, 1980). The general idea is that knowledge characteristics will likely interact with culture to influence international problem–solution exchanges.

The homogeneity or heterogeneity of language, customs, and markets may influence the probability of exchanges. Global organizations operate in regions where there is more commonality in terms of language and culture. We would expect a greater number of exchanges between work settings in different countries within the same region (e.g., Venezuela and Colombia).

Another factor would be prior ties or networks across different work settings. The greater the familiarity between two international settings about their respective personnel, practices and work activities, the more likely knowledge exchanges would occur. The ties may come about through personnel rotation, employee memberships in global professional associations, or functional dependence.

Culture, itself, should play a major role in knowledge exchanges. Explicit in the discussion of CALS are values about cooperative, open exchanges. For exchanges to occur, there needs to be some collaborative orientation. Values should support giving and seeking help regardless of position or status. Two levels of culture may facilitate or inhibit knowledge exchanges.

National culture may affect the form of exchanges. For example, we earlier suggested that experts could be used as part of a CALS to facilitate problem–solution matching. The success and role of experts would likely be affected by national culture. For example, the normative acceptance of lifetime employment in Japan may make it more likely that experts could be raised and cultivated within a single Japanese organization. Alternatively, the movement away from lifetime employment in the US may mean that cultivation of experts is more difficult for American firms. The general idea is that characteristics of the CALS will interact with the national culture to influence international problem–solution exchanges.

Additionally, organizational culture can influence exchanges. When the norms and values in an organization support collaboration and citizenship behavior, exchanges will be facilitated. The opposite also will be true.

FORMALLY DESIGNED CALS VERSUS INFORMALLY DESIGNED CALS

The existing research has focused on formally sanctioned and supported uses of CALS. We recognize it is unlikely that individual employees or even groups of employees will have the resources necessary for infrastructure (e.g., servers, cables, switches, etc.) deployment. The design issues we highlight are concerned with system uses given an existing infrastructure. For example, CALS which use Lotus Notes as the primary software piece may be altered by individual end-users. In some organizations, users have sufficient technical training to do their own Lotus Notes development. These users can create new Notes programs (i.e., applications) which are automatically replicated to other computers. Groups of users can independently identify a common topic of interest, create a discussion database, and begin sharing and storing knowledge.

Informally designed CALS represent an alternative strategy. In one study (Goodman & Darr, 1995) informal communities for learning were identified. These communities were self-designed, composed of people in common work areas, used multiple types of media for exchanges, and had strong views supporting learning. In many ways these groups avoided some of the inhibitors of problem–solution exchanges. Since they were self-designed, there were strong commitments and motivation to exchange problems and solutions. Also, since they worked in common areas, they had a common language and sets of experiences to frame problems and solutions.

The research opportunity is to explore the role of informal communities for learning in geographically distributed environments. One approach is simply to learn about frequency and types of the informal communities. In Goodman and Darr (1995), these communities were inadvertently discovered and their existence was unknown to most senior managers. How did these communities get started? What is their major function? Who are the members? Another issue is whether organizations can (and should) facilitate the development of these communities. The apparent contradiction is that these communities have developed independently of the formal system. So is it possible formally to create an environment where these communities may develop?

Related research should explore how organizations can facilitate CALS self-design without giving up centralized network control. Many organizations using Lotus Notes are currently struggling with the placement of development activities. Some believe that individual users should be empowered to create databases. These organizations centrally establish guidelines and procedures for getting databases approved and included on the network, but let individual users develop any type of application as long as it fits within the guidelines. Other organizations using Lotus Notes do all development work in a central group. End-users are given no development training, and are actively discouraged from development. The central issue is that while self-designed CALS may increase individual commitment, they may decrease organizational control. Central control may be necessary to insure effective network operation, as well as quality of network input. Research should examine the advantages and disadvantages of self-designed CALS.

UNTESTED ASSUMPTIONS

Our strategy in defining areas of opportunity for research has been to identify the features of current CALS studies and then change some of these features. Since most studies have been in single firms and in the same country, we have argued that examining exchanges between different firms or firms in different countries would open up some interesting and important areas for research.

As we conclude this identification of research opportunities, it is important to bring the reader back to the original specification of organizational learning. We argued that organizational learning occurs when: (a) problem–solution exchanges occur and are communicated to organizational members; (b) these exchanges are stored in organizational memory; and (c) there is shared interpretation about the exchanges and updating by organizational members of their experiences. Yet, most CALS research does not focus on these three features, particularly on the role of memory and shared interpretations. We feel these are the critical aspects of studying organizational learning whether one works from a technological or non-technological perspective. Below we argue that understanding these areas and the effectiveness of CALS represents new and exciting research opportunities.

If we want to increase our understanding of CALS, we need to focus on memory and storage issues, not just on exchanges. How are exchanges stored in memory? Given that memory resides in multiple locations (Walsh & Ungson, 1991), how are memories accessed and updated? From a methodological perspective, should we measure all knowledge stores or just some portion? We need new metrics for assessing how and why people access organizational memory vs initiating direct requests to others for assistance. How do we evaluate how current the memory is for solving problems?

We argued that the process by which organizational members develop shared interpretations of problem–solution exchanges is an important component of organizational learning. But this process has not been studied. One methodological challenge is to develop measures of shared interpretations. How much overlap between interpretations is required before we call it shared? How do we characterize the interpretations so that comparison across individuals is possible?

Another research challenge is assessing effectiveness of computer-aided learning systems. It seems that we want to do more than consider usage or satisfaction with CALS. The underlying assumption during the deployment of CALS is that they will contribute to organizational effectiveness. By sharing problems and solutions, organizational units do not have to reinvent what others have discovered. Sharing also can stimulate creative ideas and new applications. The question is whether CALS do improve organizational effectiveness.

One approach to this question, which is common to most technological applications in organizations, is by focusing on different levels of analysis. CALS encourage exchanges between at least two individuals. One question in this inquiry is whether and how the exchanges lead to any implementation of a new organizational practice. Another question is how the new practice relates to unit effectiveness criteria. For example, some exchanges in a service unit may impact on costs, while others impact on customer satisfaction. If the traces between exchange, practice, and outcome can be identified, another issue is how these changes at the exchange or organizational subunit level translate to changes of the organization level. Some recent research (Harris, 1994) has begun to explore the linkages among individual, subunit and organizational effectiveness changes. The task of tracing through impacts of exchanges and the linkages between exchanges across levels is an intriguing challenge for organizational researchers.

CONCLUSION

Organizational learning is an important concept for advancing organizational theory and practice. Computer-aided systems represent one approach to understanding learning processes in organizations. Our strategy has not been to focus on the technology per se, but rather to argue that the technology creates an opportunity to explore a series of important issues.

Our emphasis has been on content rather than methodology. However, it is important to acknowledge that there are many methodological challenges. Most work in CALS has been on examining exchanges between users by using interview and survey techniques. It is clear we need to explore other strategies. In terms of sampling, we need to know about non-users as well as users. We need to know more about the context within which learning occurs. What mechanisms are used? How do people switch among CALS and other transfer mechanisms? To capture these dynamics, we probably need to utilize more ethnomethodological procedures. Richer descriptions of the learning content would be an important departure from current work. In our discussion on effectiveness, we pointed out the need for a tracing methodology. How can we follow exchanges to implementations to outcomes, and then trace outcomes at individual or unit levels to organization levels?

Although our inquiry has been focused on CALS, many of the issues we examined are related to current challenges in organization research. One opportunity area we explored concerned exchanges across cultural context. Doing work in a cross-cultural context is, of course, not limited to problem–solution exchanges via CALS. There is a growing interest in developing our theoretical frameworks and understanding for organizing and conducting work in a global context. One way to advance our understanding of cross-cultural organizational behavior is to focus on tasks. Tasks provide a specific frame for understanding the role of cross-cultural issues. Investigations of CALS is an international context should contribute to our understanding of organizational learning and cross-cultural organization work.

Learning processes are fundamental to organizational work. Focusing on CALS gives us a perspective from which to understand organizational learning.

REFERENCES

Argote, L. (1993) Group and organizational learning curves: Individual, system and environmental components. *British Journal of Social Psychology*, **32,** 31–51.

Argyris, C. & Schon, D. (1978) *Organizational Learning: A Theory of Action Perspective.* Reading, MA: Addison-Wesley.

Brown, J. S. & Duguid, P. (1991) Organizational learning and communities-of-practice: Toward a unified view of working, learning and innovation. *Organization Science,* **2** (1), 40–57.

Cohen, W. M. & Levinthal, D. A. (1990) Absorptive capacity: A new perspective on learning and innovation. *Administrative Science Quarterly,* **35,** 128–152.

Constant, D., Sproull, L. & Kiesler, S. (1995) The kindness of strangers: On the usefulness of weak ties for technical advice. *Organization Science,* in press.

Darr, E. D. (1994) Partner similarity and knowledge transfer in franchised organizations. Doctoral dissertation, Graduate School of Industrial Administration, Carnegie Mellon University.

Day, G. (1994) Continuous learning about markets. *California Management Review,* 9–31.

Finholt, T. A. (1993) Outsiders on the inside: Sharing information through a computer archive. Doctoral dissertation, Department of Social and Decision Sciences, Carnegie Mellon University.

Goodman, P. S. & Darr, E. D. (1995) Computer-aided systems and communities as mechanisms for organizational learning, in review process, *MIS Quarterly.*

Harris, D. (Ed.) (1994) *Organizational Linkages: Understanding the Productivity Paradox.* Washington, DC: National Academy Press.

Hofstede, G. (1980) *Culture's Consequences: International Differences in Work Related Values.* Beverly Hills, CA: Sage.

Huber, G. P. (1991) Organizational learning: The contributing processes and the literature. *Organization Science,* **2,** 88–115.

Keller, R. & Chinta, R. (1990) International technology transfer: Strategies for success. *Academy of Management Executive,* **4,** 33–43.

Kiesler, S., Siegel, J. & McGuire, T. (1984) Social psychological aspect of computer-mediated communication. *American Psychologist,* **39,** 1123–1134.

Kiesler, S. & Sproull, L. (1987) *Computing and Change on Campus.* New York: Cambridge University Press.

Kim, D. H. (1993) The link between individual and organizational learning. *Sloan Management Review* (Fall), 37–50.

Kraut, R., Galegher, J., Fish, R. & Chalfonte, B. (1992) Task requirements and media choice in collaborative writing. *Human Computer Interaction,* **7,** 375–407.

Levitt, B. & March, J. G. (1988) Organizational learning. *Annual Review of Sociology,* **14,** 319–340.

Miner, A. & Haunschild, P. (1995) Population level learning. *Research in Organizational Behavior,* **17,** 115–166.

Nonaka, I. (1994) A dynamic theory of organizational knowledge creation. *Organization Science,* **5** (1), 14–37.

Orlikowski, W. J. (1992) The duality of technology: Rethinking the concept of technology in organizations. *Organization Science,* **3,** 398–427.

Orlikowski, W. J. (1993) Learning from notes: Organizational issues in groupware implementation. *The Information Society,* **9,** 237–250.

Rice, R. E. & Shook, D. E. (1990) Voice messaging, coordination, and communication. In J. Galegher, R. E. Kraut and C. Egido (Eds), *Intellectual Teamwork,* pp. 327–350. Hillsdale, NJ: Lawrence Erlbaum Associates.

Senge, P. (1990) *The Fifth Discipline: The Art and Practice of the Learning Organization.* New York: Doubleday Currency.

Sproull, L. & Kiesler, S. (1986) Reducing social context cues: Electronic main in organizational communication. *Management Science*, **32**, 1492–1512.

Stata, Ray (1989) Organizational learning—the key to management innovation. *Sloan Management Review* (Spring), 63–74.

Walsh, J. (1995) Managerial and organizational cognition: Notes from a trip down memory lane. *Organization Science*, **6**, 280–321.

Walsh, J. & Ungson, G. R. (1991) Organizational memory. *Academy of Management Review*, **16**, 57–91.

CHAPTER 6

Toward an Understanding of the Variety in Work Arrangements: The Organization and Labor Relationships Framework

Peter D. Sherer

University of Oregon, Eugene, OR, USA

Alternative work arrangements are on the rise. Organizations in retail sales, entertainment and financial services, and the taxicab industry hire lessees, requiring them to pay a fee to use equipment, materials or space. Organizations are now "renting" senior executives and even CEOs. In the airlines, employees have been made owners, paying them as claimants to the firm's profits and giving them voice and vote in firm matters as stockholders. Perhaps most commonly, organizations are using teams with self-management (i.e., horizontal control) rather than hierarchical control by management. The ascendance of these and other alternative arrangements—arrangements that vary from standard or modal practice in an industry or across industries—coupled with the growing awareness of the linkages between work arrangements and firm strategies and capabilities, suggest that the time is ripe to move toward a greater understanding of the variety in work arrangements.

The internal labor market (ILM) framework (see Doeringer & Piore, 1971) has been the foundation for much of the study on the variety in work arrangements, through its discussion of employee movement in and across organizations and employee pay determination. We can no longer rely on this framework, however. The subject of the ILM literature

Trends in Organizational Behavior, Volume 3. Edited by C. L. Cooper and D. M. Rousseau
© 1996 John Wiley & Sons Ltd

has been the structure of standard or modal employment relationships. There are, however, many alternatives to these employment relationships and to employment relationships altogether.

Studying the variety in work arrangements, therefore, calls for a broader perspective, one that addresses non-standard variants of employment and *non*-employment relationships involving labor in organizations. Pieces to this greater variety are suggested by various literatures. Literature on the externalization of ILMs (Pfeffer & Baron, 1988) discusses how employees are taken partially outside of organizations; literature on the further internalization of ILMs discusses how employees are taken deeper inside organizations through the use of teams (Williamson, 1985). Principal–agent literature on sharecropping discusses franchise-like arrangements that are used to contract labor in as non-employees (Allen, 1985; Newberry & Stiglitz, 1979; Sappington, 1991). Literature on property rights in organizations discusses arrangements in which those who do the labor are owners, not employees (Williamson, 1980).

What is missing is a framework with the robustness to capture these pieces to the variety and that has the additional capacity to capture those arrangements which have not been discovered or are only imaginable. That is where a framework I have developed (Sherer, 1993) on organization and labor relationships (OLR) comes in. With this framework, I show that underlying the variety in work arrangements are three distinct forms of agency, embodied in three organizations and labor relationships (OLRs): (a) when labor operates as an agent under the direct control of an organization it is in an *employment relationship*; (b) when labor operates as a quasi-agent in that is only partially under the control of an organization it is in a *contracting-in relationship*; or (c) when labor operates both as an agent and an owner with control in the organization it is in an *ownership relationship*.

By focusing on these three fundamental relationships, the OLR framework serves as a foundation that provides both unity and division to the study of the variety in work arrangements. It additionally directs research in two directions. One is in calling for a neo-institutional theory of work arrangements through writing a grammar to express actual and imaginable forms of work arrangements (Salancik & Leblebici, 1988). And, since form and function are inextricably linked, the OLR framework melds with the resource-based approach to strategy (Barney, 1991; Grant, 1991; Rumelt, 1984, 1987; Wernerfelt, 1984) in calling for research that addresses how work arrangements: (a) vary in the degree to which they are imitable; (b) are part of firm differentiation and imitation strategies; and (c) are central to the development of organizational capabilities through their effects on such internal assets as the dedication and fluidity of labor, human capital structures, and organizational learning and absorptive capacities.

The paper is ordered as follows. The pieces to the variety, including the ILM literature, are first addressed. The OLR framework is then presented. The OLR framework is then applied to taxicab organizations, law firms and corporations in the aim of showing its robustness, its "grammatical" implications, and value in establishing linkages between work arrangements and strategy and firm capabilities. The conclusion discusses how the OLR framework provides a new perspective for understanding the variety in work arrangements and, in so doing, offers many opportunities for micro, meso and macro organizational researchers.

PIECES TO THE VARIETY

The internal labor market (ILM) framework (Doeringer & Piore, 1971), the foundation for organizational studies on the structure of work arrangements, uses the metaphor of labor being internalized and hence insiders in a firm or occupation as compared to those who are outsiders to a firm or occupation. An internal labor market exists when labor inside a firm or occupation faces a different set of rules and is insulated from the competitive forces of the external labor market. Doeringer and Piore (1971) argue that the advantage of ILMs for organizations is that they allow labor to be allocated more efficiently than would be the case if they had to rely on outsiders from the external labor market and that the advantage for employees is that they are buffered from the vicissitudes of external competitive forces.

Employment in firm ILMs involves strict rules about entry, promotion and rewards within an organization. Those who are allowed entry inside the organization have an advantage over those individuals who are outside of it in that promotions and rewards are given to insiders. These employees work under the direct control or authority of a superior.

Employment in occupational ILMs is characterized by strong entry barriers into the ILM coupled with regulated movement across organizations. Employees move from employment with one organization to another organization along a structured path. A craft union or professional association regulates both entry and movement from one organization to another.

The degree to which individuals are internalized in a firm or occupational OLM is linked to their level of commitment. Those strongly internalized in a firm ILM have high commitment to that organization; those strongly internalized in an occupational ILM have high commitment to that occupation.

Those not fully inside a firm or occupational ILM are in a partially structured ILM or are outsiders in an unstructured (secondary) labor market (Althauser & Kalleberg, 1981). Those outside of ILMs are argued to be in casualized or informal labor markets. In the ILM framework, it is argued that little if any structure or pattern to the relationship exists between an organization and labor when it is outside of an ILM. Behaviorally, those outside a firm or occupational ILM are argued to have little or no commitment to either a firm or an occupation.

The firm and occupational ILMs capture the standard or modal employment relationships for what were two of the most common types of jobs: the firm ILM for the blue-collar jobs in manufacturing; the occupational ILM for blue-collar jobs in the skilled and the semi-skilled trades. In work by Althauser and Kalleberg (1981), these ILMs were broadened to capture aspects of managerial and professional employment.

But broadening these ILMs does not capture the variety in work arrangements that was discussed at the beginning of this paper. They are alternative work arrangements because they depart from these ILMs.

Pfeffer and Baron (1988) bring to light several alternative work arrangements by literally turning the notion of an ILM inside out, focusing on how work is externalized, and how this process transforms standard employment relationships into alternative work arrangements. They argue that work is externalized by: (a) the externalization of control that occurs through the use of market control as a substitute for organizational or administrative control; (b) the externalization of place that occurs through having work done outside of centralized work places; and (c) the externalization of time that occurs through the dissolution of rules that specify standard hours at work. These externalizing forces move labor from the internal labor market to somewhat outside of it. Pfeffer and Baron suggest that these externalizing forces are advantageous to organizations in achieving lower labor costs, attracting and retaining labor, and having a flexible workforce in the sense that labor can readily be added and dropped.

Pfeffer and Baron argue that the process of externalization captures, for example, those work arrangements in which individuals are contracted in to do work but are outside of that organization in terms of who ultimately has control over them (Davis-Blake & Uzzi, 1993; Pfeffer & Baron, 1988). The problem with their argument here is that, if we simply focus, as they do, on these arrangements being externalized, we lose sight that there is much more to them, that they are not necessarily casual and unstructured and that, in fact, they may be even more structured than internalized arrangements. When labor is "outside" of an organization, it still has a relationship with an organization, only it is not that of employment.

Williamson (1985) further expands the range of alternative arrangements within the ILM framework by discussing how greater internalization of ILMs occurs through teams. Williamson argues that, when teams are internalized but members can be interchanged with those from outside the team, only a primitive team exists. These teams are primitive in that team members need each other to perform tasks (e.g., two individuals are needed to pick up a board that one alone could not), but there is a lack of permanence or interdependency among members because they are substitutable (fungible) with one another. When teams are further internalized in that team members are not fungible with those from outside of the team and instead an intact team is needed for learning and synergies to occur, relational teams exist. These teams involve long-standing relationships and strong interdependency among members.

Williamson has captured some types of teams, but not all teams are internalized. While Williamson's argument predicts, for example, that internalization in primitive teams results in only individuals leaving and that internalization in relational teams results in virtually no one leaving, his argument does not explain those teams in which the members leave an organization en masse. There are also teams whose membership is in two firms, joined through alliances, whose organizational attachments are at the interface of the two organizations.

Pfeffer and Baron (1988) and Williamson (1985) take the ILM framework as far as it can go, but it is unable to address the full range of variety in work arrangements. The problem is that the ILM framework is based solely on a metaphor about the insideness vs outsideness of employment—those relationships in which labor works on behalf of an organization (typically the corporation and referred to as the principal) as its agent, bearing a fiduciary obligation of loyalty to the principal, pursuing profits on its behalf (Klein & Coffee, 1990).

This metaphor only touches on important underlying properties of work arrangements that involve *non*-employment relationships, raising questions but never really answering them. Is the externalization of work central to understanding leasing arrangements? Is it internalization or externalization when employees move from guaranteed pay to pay like owners as residual claimants? Is internalization or externalization central to understanding ownership by labor through voice and vote? While it is possible to fashion answers to these and other such questions that suggest the centrality of the processes of internalization and externalization, they are not convincing. These processes are not central to what generates these arrangements.

The result is that the ILM framework cannot fundamentally address what makes work arrangements similar or different. To see this point more clearly, consider the case of lessees in taxicab organizations. The ILM framework views them as being in a partially internalized or external labor market since they have little of the internalized movement up or across taxicab organizations. However, the leasing arrangement reflects a structured or patterned relationship between the organization and its driver in that the transaction between the two has been formalized and is repeated for extended periods of time. It simply is not internalized in an employment relationship. Consider too those who make partner in professional service firms. In the ILM perspective, making partner is equated with moving up an internal labor market (Wholey, 1985). But making partner confers property rights in the organization while getting a promotion does not. Equating the two clouds over what are very real differences in the relationship between the organization and its labor.

The agency theory literature on sharecropping (e.g., Allen, 1985; Newberry & Stiglitz, 1979; Sappington, 1991) looks at arrangements that parallel employment but additionally addresses non-employment relationships. Agency theorists interested in sharecropping address commission employment as share contracts (i.e., a landlord and tenant agree on a split of the revenues from crops) and hourly or straight salary employment as wage contracts (i.e., a landlord agrees upfront to pay a tenant a fixed or flat rate for tending to fields). They address sharecropping arrangements that parallel non-employment through leasing or "franchise fees" (Sappington, 1991).[1] In these arrangements, lessees as tenants pay a fixed rent to the lessor to work the land, taking all the proceeds from it, and thus acting as residual claimants.

Leasing arrangements are, for the most part, not regarded as employment relationships in US courts (Morris, 1983).[2] Courts have reasoned that a lessee is less subject to the control of a lessor than an employee is under the control of an employer and therefore that leasing arrangements are not employment relationships. Instead, courts have argued that most such arrangements reflect instances where there may be some agency but that the agent is more independent and therefore a contractor with the organization. Such lessees are legally viewed as independent contractors—that is, they are under contract to work for an organization and may be its partial agents but they are not its employees (Morris, 1983).

---

[1] Among organizational researchers, Eisenhardt (1988) used agency theory to study why employees in retail services are paid a salary or commission; Peterson (1992) additionally looked at the determinants of salary plus commission systems. These studies did not address leasing.

[2] It is important to distinguish between leasing and employment leasing. The latter occurs when an employer "leases" or transfers employees to another organization in order to have that organization administer employee benefits.

While sharecropping is a useful context in which to see the use of franchising-like arrangements, it too provides only some of the variety in work arrangements. Since sharecropping involves one party holding ownership over the land, agency theorists interested in sharecropping do not address those arrangements in which labor co-owns and co-operates the land. Such ownership arrangements are not only possible, Russell (1991) has documented their existence in a number of types of organizations.

Williamson (1980) addresses two distinct ownership or property rights modes in which those who do the labor are the owners. One, entrepreneurial ownership, involves the majority of the capital (e.g., equipment, financial assets) of an organization being held separately by owner-operators who join together in loose combinations. Since these arrangements typically involve cost sharing but not revenue sharing, they are referred to as involving "eat what you kill" or "every man/woman for himself/herself". A second, communal ownership, involves owner-operators costs and revenues in varying degrees. This mode exists today in professional partnerships such as in law or accounting firms. There, partners share ownership and work in the firm.

The above literatures suggest a number of important pieces to the variety in work arrangements. As summarized in Table 6.1, the range of this variety is from those standard employment relationships that have been the focus of the ILM literature (Doeringer & Piore, 1971; Althauser & Kalleberg, 1981), to the externalized arrangements discussed by Pfeffer and Baron (1988) and the internalized teams discussed by Williamson (1985), to sharecropping arrangements involving franchise-like fees discussed by agency theorists (Allen, 1985;

Table 6.1   Pieces to the variety

Literature	Type of work arrangements
ILM	Standard/modal employment relationships (firm and occupational ILM)
Externalization of ILMs	Externalized employment (e.g., contract workers)
Internalization of ILMs	Internalized employment through teams
Principal–Agent	Sharecropping through franchise-like fees
Ownership/Property rights	Communal (e.g., professional partnerships) Entrepreneurial (e.g., eat what you kill)

Newberry & Stiglitz, 1979), to the ownership modes discussed by Williamson (1980).

This variety calls for a framework that can both bring together and differentiate among work arrangements. The objective of the OLR framework is to serve as a foundation that can provide both unity and division to our understanding of the variety in work arrangements.

THE OLR FRAMEWORK

The notion of agency is fundamental to understanding the variety in work arrangements that were discussed at the beginning of this paper and in the last section. Agency is a legal concept which refers to those situations in which a principal authorizes another party as agent to act on his/her behalf (typically in pursuing profits), subject to the control of the principal (see Klein & Coffee, 1990; Sells, 1976; Steffen, 1977).

At the heart of the legal concept of agency is the issue of control. A principal has the right of direct control over an agent, what we typically refer to as the authority relationship (Simon, 1951), because the agent acts as a representative of the firm and the organization is liable for the torts of the agent.[3] The agent either explicitly or implicitly takes an oath of fiduciary loyalty to the firm, which is usually interpreted to mean that the agent must attempt to maximize profits on behalf of the firm. For example, the agent has a duty to avoid selling products or services for personal gain if the employer would lose profits by the agent's selling activities (Klein & Coffee, 1990).

This standard form of agency assumes a principal has direct control over an agent. As shown in Figure 6.1, agency can take different forms, reflecting other modes of control (Sherer, 1993). Quasi-agency takes place when a principal has only partial control over an agent and/or the agent is only working partially on behalf the principal. For example, with franchise-like arrangements, the principal does not have as much control over the agent as when he/she directly employs the agent nor is the agent working fully on behalf of the interests of the principal. Mutual agency takes place when an agent is subject to the control of the organization but at the same time the agent is the principal and therefore has control over other agents. For example, with partnerships, partners are principals but they are agents too; as agents they are subject to the control of other principals.

---

[3] Much of the view of a principal–agent relationship comes from applying the Doctrine of Respondeat Superior and the notion of master–servant relationships to determining the liability of a master for the torts of his/her servant (Gorman, 1976).

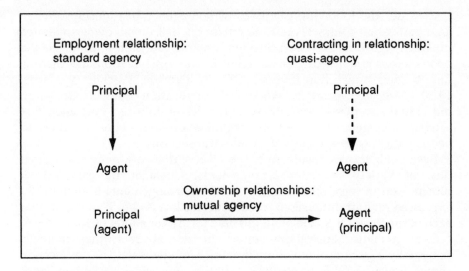

Figure 6.1 Agency characterizations of the three organization–labor relationships

Employment relationships embody the standard form of agency. An employee as agent works on behalf of an employer who as principal has rights of control over employees within limits. Translating this legal concept into behavioral terms, Simon (1951) states that employment gives an employer the right to authority over an employee within a zone of acceptable tasks and responsibilities.

Contracting-in relationships embody quasi-agency. Individuals are hired by the organization, but it has limited legal rights of authority over the individual and/or the individual is working on behalf of the organization only in a limited sense. Individuals operating as quasi-agents thus have more independence from the organizations to which they are contracted in.

Ownership relationships embody mutual agency. These relationships are complex in that owner-operators are both principals and agents. As principals, they exercise control over agents; and, as agents, they are subject to the control of the other principals.

Salancik and Leblebici (1988) argue that a framework that seeks to show order to a class of institutional arrangements has to be able to say not only what variety belongs in the framework but what variety is outside of or invariant to it. The OLR framework dictates the exclusion of those arrangements in which there is not an agency relationship between an organization and labor. Such arrangements do not represent organizational relationships with labor.

Consider the following examples of non-agency relationships. When an organization contracts out to purchase goods from an owner-operator in which control is exercised through a market decision to purchase the goods, labor is not acting as an agent for the organization and there is only a sales transaction (Simon, 1951; Williamson, Wachter & Harris, 1975). Also, for example, when an organization rents a car to an individual and places restrictions on the driver only as a customer, that leasing arrangement is not an organization and labor relationship because there is no agency, only a sales transactions.

Even with this exclusion rule, the OLR framework suggests a great deal of variety in work arrangements. Consider the simplest of illustrations in which the variation in work arrangements is analytically expressed on four dimensions, each with two levels (24). That means that each of the three OLRs yields 16 possible forms, for a total of 48.

Such analytic illustrations show, in the abstract, that there is potentially a great deal of variety in work arrangements. The next section shows how the OLR framework captures the actual variety in work arrangements.

APPLICATIONS OF THE OLR FRAMEWORK

Taxicab Organizations

The study of taxicab organizations and taxicab drivers is a particularly interesting application of the OLR framework because all drivers do the same activity—drive cabs. What go unseen are the different work arrangements that drivers have with organizations, what other arrangements might be possible, and what the linkages of the work arrangements are to the strategies and capabilities of these organizations.

Sherer, Rogovsky, and Wright (1995) used the OLR framework to examine the forms of the OLRs that taxicab organizations have with drivers. These different work arrangements are shown in Table 6.2. Drivers are in employment relationships in which they are under the authority of the organization and get an hourly wage or a commission. Drivers are in contracting-in relationships in which they are less subject to the authority of the organization and their pay is based on their claim to the residual from passenger fees minus the leasing fee they are charged by the taxicab organization. Drivers are in ownership relationships in which they have control over organizational decisions (e.g., the purchasing of advertising) but have to abide by rules the organization has for drivers, and their pay is based on their claim to the residual from passenger fees minus membership fees they pay to the organization.

Table 6.2 Forms of the OLRs in taxicab organizations

Relationship (form)	Type of agency control	Financial claims
Employment (hourly or commission)	Standard agency	Hourly wage (fixed claim) or hourly wage plus commission (fixed plus variable claim)
Contracting in (leasing)	Quasi-agency	Passenger fees–leasing fee (residual claimant)
Ownership (eat what you kill)	Mutual agency	Passenger fees– membership fees (residual claimant)

The OLR framework adds to our understanding of the variety in work arrangements in the taxicab industry in several ways. First, it shows that employment relationships are only one of three possible relationships between organizations and their labor. Since the modal practice in the taxicab industry today is contracting in through leasing, it also is an instance in which the employment relationship is the alternative work arrangement (Fragin, 1994; Sherer, Rogovsky & Wright, 1995).

The OLR framework also suggests that differentiating work arrangements solely on the basis of payment structures, as many principal–theorists do, loses out on information and may be misleading. Both lessees and owners in taxicab organizations have claims to the residual from fees they generate minus costs they have to the organization. What differentiates these residual claimants is the type of agency that they have with their organizations: owners have mutual agency with their organizations; lessees have quasi-agency with their organizations.

The OLR framework sensitizes us to those arrangements which are imaginable or feasible but are only rarely or not all observed (Salancik & Leblebici, 1988). Ownership relationships among taxicab drivers occur as loose combinations, with drivers limiting the amount of joint governance they undertake, and their financial claims coming in the form of an "eat what you kill" pay system. Yet, an alternative might be for drivers to have tight partnerships or communal ownership in which drivers share their pay. Contracting in through leasing is typically expressed through relatively short-term contracts of a day to a week long in which the driver rents the car as an operating lease (i.e., the driver pays a fee to rent the car, but the rental fee does not go toward the purchase of the car). Yet, an alternative might be to have long-term contracts in which the driver rented the car through a capital lease (i.e., rental fees would go toward the purchase of the car) rather than an operating lease.

Determining why these alternative arrangements are not observed is clearly an important question for research. However, traditional research approaches will not be very useful in studying them. Since these arrangements are rarely or not at all observed, they are difficult to test statistically for their advantages or disadvantages. Thus, our understanding of them rests with conducting case or "outlier" studies of the few observed instances of them and in developing grammatical rules and theories to explain both their existence and non-existence.

The more frequently observed forms of the OLRs, however, have legal implications that are important in drawing out their capabilities (Sherer, 1993). The key point is that organizations can legally exercise a great deal of control with employees, are legally able to exercise considerably less control with lessees in contracting-in relationships, and exercise joint control with owners; however, organizations have greater costs and less flexibility with employment than the other two OLRs because they have to abide by employment protections such as those on the rates of pay that are specified in the Fair Labor Standards Act.

Given these legal implications, three linkages stand out between the forms of the OLRs and strategy and capabilities. One is that hourly employees give organizations a capability for liquidity. This internal liquidity is needed to provide services that require reliability, such as picking up children from school. This capability rises because organizations legally have a great deal of direct control over hourly employees and do not have to be concerned with their incentives leading them to be motivated in ways that run counter to the organization's commands; lessees and owners are not subject to such control and have incentives that may put them in conflict with the organization (e.g., overcharging a client). A second is that employment links to standards for doing things that speak to quality. This capability arises because managerial activities aimed at insuring standards can only be accomplished legally through the direct control that comes with employment relationships. It is only with employees that an organization can, for example, tell drivers how to dress and how to conduct themselves with passengers. The third is that contracting in through leasing gives organizations the capability to exploit market opportunities inexpensively and quickly. Lessees allow organizations to have this fluid capability because they impose low fixed labor costs on organizations and drivers have a great deal of motivation to get spot transactions (e.g. picking up passengers on the street) because they start in the red.

Taxicab organizations have been using what have been alternative arrangements in other industries for quite some time. For example, contracting in through leasing has been used in the taxicab industry since at least the seventeenth century, with hackney (i.e., large and heavy wooden carriages) owners contracting in with "hacks", leasing them vehicles for fees; its modern history dates to the Great Depression and "cut-rate" operators who hired lessees who charged rates that significantly undercut competitors (Gilbert & Samuels, 1982).

Given the long history the taxicab industry has with alternative work arrangements, insights from it can be used to examine trends in the use of those arrangements in other industries. Leasing, for example, is now used with home-remodelling salespeople who purchase and put in roofing and siding they purchase from their firm (Carlson, 1991), financial stockbrokers who rent space and the name of the firm (Antilla, 1993), and female and male bar dancers who pay a fee to the bar to rent space to dance and make tips (Phalon, 1993). Our (Sherer, Rogovsky & Wright, 1995) results suggest that leasing will continue to grow because it provides organizations with fluid assets and thus contributes to fluid capabilities for quickly and inexpensively exploiting market opportunities (Sherer, 1993). Moreover, most of these leasing arrangements are highly imitable because of their simplicity and they therefore spread easily and quickly through an industry or inter-organizational field. However, our results suggest that the growth of leasing is constrained when an organization requires a dedicated capability for liquidity in its workforce or is concerned with the quality of its product or service.

Law Firms

Law firms are organized as professional partnerships, not as corporations. As professional partnerships, they have no external stockholders, only internal stockholders composed of lawyers who are members of their firms. While it might be expected that these firms would have virtually all lawyers as partners, only a few firms are organized in that way.[4] Instead, most firms have a number of different work arrangements for their lawyers and the way in which organizations mix these arrangements speaks to the capabilities they have.

As shown in Table 6.3, Sherer (1995) used the OLR framework to address the forms of the OLRs for lawyers in large law firms. Lawyers in these firms are in ownership relationships in which they are partners. Their role as partners makes them the stockholders in their firms,

---

[4] Given that it is very rare to find a law firm with only partners, Huseyin Leblebici (University of Illinois at Urbana-Champaign) and I are studying those few instances of this arrangement and why it is not more common.

Table 6.3 Forms of the OLRs in law firms

Relationship (form)	Type of agency	Financial claims
Ownership (partners)	Mutual agency	Share on profits (residual claimant = equity holder)
Employment (associates)	Standard agency	Annual salary (fixed claimant = debt holder)
Contracting in (Of Counsel)	Quasi-agency	Payment per case, client fee-leasing fee, retainer

entitling them to voice and vote in firm matters, and pay as residual claimants to the firm's income (payment varies from seniority based, to merit based, to every one taking what he/she generates in revenue). Lawyers in these firms are in employment relationships in which they are referred to as associates. Their role as employees places them under the direct control of partners, having little to no control in firm matters, and their compensation largely taking the form of a guaranteed salary. Lawyers in these firms are in contracting-in relationships in which they are referred to as Of Counsel (Wagner, 1986). They are only partially subject to its control and ordinarily have little in the way of voice or vote in firm matters. The American Bar Association requires that, to be an Of Counsel, a lawyer must have close, continuing and personal relationships with firms (Wren & Glascock, 1990). Of Counsel are hired on a case-by-case basis or retainer to provide knowledge and expertise and they may rent space from the organization and work part of the time for it and part of the time for other organizations.

These forms of the OLRs directly link to two types of capabilities in law firms. Partners have been historically dedicated to their firms in the sense that they stayed in one firm and committed themselves to learning specifically about it and its clients while bearing the negative and positive risks of the organization (Allen & Sherer, 1995; Sherer, 1995). As dedicated assets, partners contributed to the dedicated capabilities these firms needed to maintain and foster long-term client relationships (Allen & Sherer, 1995; Sherer, 1993). Associates and Of Counsel are more readily "acquired" and discharged. The fluidity of these human assets gives firms the capability to respond flexibly to market opportunities (Allen & Sherer, 1995; Sherer, 1993).

Firms also mix the OLRs in different combinations to achieve other more complex or combinatorial capabilities (Sherer, 1993). The most critical combinations involve teams of partners as owners and associates as employees. These teams allow firms to leverage their human assets in a way that is analogous to firms leveraging their financial assets: firms leverage financial assets through the residual claims (i.e., financial claims reflecting the residual payment from revenues minus costs) of equity holders relative to the fixed claims (i.e., financial claims that call for a predetermined level of payment that does not vary with revenues or costs) of debt holders, with the ratio of debt to equity referring to the leverage ratio and reflecting the financial capital structure for a firm; firms leverage human assets through the residual claims of partners as equity holders relative to the fixed claims (here, in the form of guaranteed yearly salaries) of associates as debt holders, with the debt to equity ratio referring to the human capital structure for a firm.

Two distinct firm capabilities stood out when the leverage ratio for principal offices of firms was interacted with the specialization (in terms of legal services) ratio for these offices in order to predict the high-end client billing rates (firms use high-end billing rates to signal where they stand in the market for legal services). First, principal offices with the highest high billing rates had capabilities built around a rare and tightly controlled human capital structure. Such offices had low leverage ratios and a highly specialized expertise. Second, those firms with the second highest billing rates had capabilities built around leveraging on the basis of economies of scale and scope. Such offices were highly leveraged but were multispecialized, offering one-stop shopping legal services.

These capabilities are difficult to imitate. In those firms that do not leverage associates very heavily and are highly specialized, the knowledge of partners stays in the firm and the expertise is rare. The work arrangements in these firms act as isolating mechanisms (Rumelt, 1984, 1987)—means by which firms keep invisible or closely guarded what makes them distinctive—through not letting go of many associates and making sure that partners remain dedicated to the firm. In those firms that leverage highly and have multispecialty firms such that they provide one-stop shopping for legal services, they build their capabilities through leveraging on the basis of economies of scale and competing on variety and price together. While leveraging is easier when a firm is highly specialized in that templates or boilerplates can be used to impart partner knowledge efficiently to associates, these firms have learned to effectively leverage while being multispecialized.

The leveraging strategies used by these and other principal offices assume that associates are debt holders with "options" to become equity holders. This assumption has been formalized into the up-or-out system, dominant for much of the twentieth century in law firms (Galanter & Palay, 1991; Gilson & Mnookin, 1988), part of what is called the "Cravath System" for managing lawyers. Up-or-out involved hiring only associates on track to make it up to partner and either moving them up to partner or moving them out of the firm.

Law firms and other professional partnerships have begun to do what firms in other industries have always done with employees—not give them the option to become owners. The trend away from up-or-out started in the early 1980s when a few highly prestigious firms began to formalize the status of senior attorneys—lawyers who were in the up-or-out system, did not make it up to partner, and were continued as "permanent" employees (Galanter & Palay, 1991; Gilson & Mnookin, 1988). Then, toward the mid 1980s, other prestigious firms began the adoption of staff attorneys—lawyers not on the up-or-out track, hired on fixed-term employment contracts (Galanter & Palay, 1991; Gilson & Mnookin, 1988).

Sherer and Lee (1995) have investigated what imitation strategies explain the spread of these alternative (for law firms) arrangements. While institutional theorists argue that organizations imitate other organizations' practices to promote their social fitness (see DiMaggio & Powell, 1983; Meyer & Rowan, 1977; Tolbert & Zucker, 1983), we argued and found support that organizations imitate other organizations in departing from industry standards in order to stay in step with the competition—what we refer to as "strategic imitation". Our support for the notion of strategic imitation came from finding with a sample of over 300 major offices of large US law firms that offices imitate on the basis of similarity in size or cohort of other offices in their city, not, as institutionalists would claim, on the basis of other offices being prestigious or larger.

These organizations engage in strategic imitation because it allows them to use a work arrangement, experiment with it, and/or have the option of implementing it on a larger scale at a later point in time and gain capabilities from it. When such imitation runs its course and spreads through the population of organizations in an industry (assuming the innovation is imitable), the work arrangement may no longer offer capabilities that are distinct or appropriable and it may create resource scarcities (e.g., in the 1980s, up-or-out resulted in the demand by major law firms for lawyers straight out of law school exceeding the supply of these lawyers). When this happens, an organization or group of organizations engages in strategic differentiation of an alternative work arrangement. Such differentiation may arise through adaptation or the birth of organizations with different arrangements.

The use by law firms of these alternative arrangements moves them closer to those work arrangements that were traditionally found in corporate entities. The result is that some lawyers become salaried employees with no option to become partners and their organizations have added hierarchy. The irony of this trend is that corporations are moving toward work arrangements that involve partnership and lean hierarchy.

Departures from Standard Employment Relationships in Corporations

Corporations are moving away from standard employment relationships involving firm ILMs and moving toward ownership and contracting relationships. The trend toward ownership has been broadly hailed as an effort by firms to create "partnerships" with their workforces. The aim of this movement is to build dedicated capabilities in organizations through the acquisition by their workforces of firm-specific knowledge and skills along with their attitudinal dedication. The trend toward contracting-in relationships in corporate entities has been viewed suspiciously as an effort to break implicit employment contracts that favored long-term tenure and promotions in firm ILMs. The aim of this movement is to gain the fluid capabilities of flexibility and outside knowledge produced by the ready movement of labor in and out of organizations.

As shown in Table 6.4, there have been two major components to the movement toward ownership in corporations. One is that organizations are using gain sharing, profit sharing and other forms of pay-at-risk that make employees more like owners. The second is that organizations are using horizontal control through teams to replace hierarchical control and thus are giving employees something of the mutual agency that partners as owners have.

Legal (Klein & Coffee, 1990) and agency theoretic (Milgrom & Roberts, 1992) arguments about ownership rights and control suggest that pay-at-risk and teams are complementary, reflecting a risk–control relationship.

Table 6.4 Departures from standard employment relationships in corporations

Toward ownership relationships	Toward contracting-in relationships
1. Payment at risk like residual claimants	1. Independent contractors or quasi-outside consultants
2. Horizontal control through teams	2. Rent-an-executive (e.g., rented CEOs)
	3. Contracted retirees

The argument is that, just as owners as residual claimants take risks and have a right of control over their actions, employees who become like residual claimants and take risks should have rights of control over their actions. Reflecting these arguments, with a sample of close to 500 corporate entities, Sherer and Lee (1994) found cross-sectional evidence that the use of payment-at-risk is tied to the use of teams.

This complementarity rule has important implications for organizations. It suggests that risk cannot be introduced without giving a workforce greater control in management and strategy. When there is a lack of complementarity such that the workforce is asked to take risks without control, this rule suggests a workforce will perceive that they are being taken advantage of, not empowered. When there is a lack of complementarity such that a workforce is given control without having to take risks, this rule suggests the workforce will have freedom but only a limited sense of responsibility for the consequences of their actions.

As shown also in Table 6.4, contracting-in relationships too are emerging and becoming part of the way that corporations operate. Firms like IBM (Johnston, 1995) have been substituting independent contractors or quasi-outside consultants for employees. In other cases, firms have gone so far as to "rent" senior executives and even CEOs (Hogg, 1989; Machan, 1990), putting them on fixed-term contracts. In still other cases, firms like IBM have contracted in their retirees (Johnston, 1995).

Organizations gain in a number of ways through these arrangements. Contracting-in relationships can give organizations a ready flow of knowledge with low fixed costs, thus giving them the fluid assets that provide flexible capabilities. When such arrangements involve contracted retirees with firm-specific human capital (Becker, 1975), they additionally provide firms with the dedicated assets needed for dedicated capabilities. By infusing external knowledge into their stock of internal knowledge, these arrangements also provide organizations with a powerful means to enhance their absorptive learning capacities (Cohen & Levinthal, 1990).

It is unclear whether the movements toward ownership and contracting reflect a more fundamental transformation in corporate entities. What is clear is that corporate entities are adopting elements of ownership, that they may be required to adopt more elements of ownership if the risk they are asking their workforces to take ultimately means they will have to give them more control, that firms are substituting contracting in for employment in order to gain fluid capabilities, that they additionally gain dedicated capabilities when those contracted in are retirees of the firm, and that firms absorb and learn more when they use those contracted in.

There are additionally key questions to be answered concerning the imitation of these work arrangements. One such key question concerns why firms differentiated themselves strategically through these work arrangements and why as well as how has the strategic imitation of these work arrangements unfolded. Another key question has to do with whether these work arrangements are imitable. They can be "seen" and in that sense they can be copied by competitors; however, it may be difficult to "transport" them in that their implementation may not carry from one local environment to another.

CONCLUSION

The OLR framework shows that very different industries—having very different technologies, legal forms (e.g., partnerships vs corporations) and occupations—have variants of the same organization and labor relationships. These variants of the OLRs show too the robustness of the OLR framework and provide interesting contrasts. Ownership in law firms means there are tight combinations and partners share at least some portion of profits; ownership in taxicab organizations means very loose combinations in which profits are not shared at all. Employment as associates in law firms provides an option to ownership but with a term limit that calls for movement up or out; employment in taxicab organizations does not involve any direct option for ownership. Contracting in in law firms is required to be a continuous and personal relationship; contracting in through leasing usually means the parties have a fleeting and transactional relationship.

The OLR framework has important implications for the way we view and study work arrangements as compared with our current view and study of them. Through everyday conversation, government publications, newspaper articles and the like, we have come to view employment as *the* way in which people work. This social discourse reflects how we think about work arrangements, how we study them, and what public policy objectives we have in mind with them. We say that people are employed (when they are also contracted in or owners doing the labor), government statistics refer to those in contracted-in or ownership relationships as the employed, we narrow our studies to only the employees in organizations, and labor laws are really employment laws for they cover only those who work in organizations as employees.

By suggesting that we abandon the habit of viewing employment as the way in which people work, the OLR framework calls for us to depart from the research that has been done on work arrangements. Instead of treating work arrangements as "there to be studied", it requires that we take these institutions more seriously, showing a concern for their institutional details and forms, and ultimately in building a neo-institutional theory of work arrangements by writing a grammar to express the actual and imaginable forms of work arrangements (Salancik & Leblebici, 1988). Instead of simply doing empirical comparisons of extant work arrangements, the OLR framework forces us to address theoretically why certain seemingly feasible arrangements are rarely or never observed and to conduct case or "outlier" studies of these rarely observed arrangements. Instead of focusing simply on work arrangements' effects on such far-removed consequences for labor as firm profits, the OLR framework calls for us to uncover the linkages that resource-based theorists (Barney, 1991; Grant, 1991; Rumelt, 1984, 1987; Wernerfelt, 1984) suggest work arrangements have to have: (a) patterns of strategic differentiation and imitation among organizations; (b) such internal assets as the dedication and fluidity of labor, human capital structures, and organizational learning and absorptive capacities; and (c) how these internal assets act as sources of capabilities; and (d) what the effects of work arrangements, internal assets and their attendant capabilities are on such ultimate outcomes as firm profits and the sustainability of these profits (i.e. rents).

This research strategy, while macro in orientation, has direct implications for micro-level research and the need to take account of context (Cappelli & Sherer, 1991). Micro-level research on attitudes and behavior mirrored the ILM literature, looking inside standard or modal employment relationships. The research strategy proposed here suggests that research on attitudes and behaviors is no longer the sole province of employment relationships and that the context of these micro-level outcomes needs to be expanded to capture those attitudes and behaviors embedded in non-standard employment relationships, contracting-in relationships, and ownership relationships. It further suggests that the study of such outcomes as *employee* satisfaction, *employee* commitment, or *employee* turnover has a built-in context, a built-in set of biases as to what outcome is important, and what direction of the outcome variable is favored. The research strategy proposed here thus forces micro-level researchers to conceptualize and develop measures that assess attitudes and behaviors that traverse all three OLRs.

This research strategy calls out to micro-level researchers to consider the macro context and has specific implications for meso-level research on work arrangements. First, it suggests we need meso research to address whether work arrangements as macro structures actually have their putative effects on micro outcomes (Cappelli & Sherer, 1991).

While researchers and corporate planners assume that such effects occur, we know that macro-level structures may not lead to the expected micro-level outcomes and in fact may lead to quite unintended outcomes (Cappelli & Sherer, 1990). Second and related, it suggests that micro research can play an integral role in our understanding of the imitability of work arrangements. Micro research will be especially important in telling us if differences in the implementation of work arrangements or the heterogeneity of local or internal environments of organizations result in work arrangements not being imitable because they have different effects across organizations. Third, it suggests we need meso research to further establish how the presence or absence of complementarity rules underlying different forms of work arrangements link to micro-level outcomes. Such research will be able to tell us, for example, what happens when a work arrangement has a complementary risk and control relationship. Fourth, it suggests meso-level bridges in the network literature between micro (i.e. individual-to-individual) and macro perspectives (i.e. organization-to-organization), since many of the networks that are work arrangements occur at the meso level. These networks involve organizations and individuals who are contracted in.

The research called for by the OLR framework is not the easy road to take. It requires that organizational researchers search out work arrangements and learn their institutional details, seek out rules for expressing extant and imaginable forms of work arrangements, and explore how forms of the OLRs and their grammatical rules relate to internal assets and organizational capabilities. It also requires that we come to a greater understanding of imitation and differentiation strategies that firms employ with work arrangements and what makes a work arrangement truly imitable. It additionally requires taking meso or micro-macro linkages seriously. Nonetheless, I believe this long, sometimes bumpy, and hopefully winding road is well worth taking. By providing us with a new perspective on the variety in work arrangements, it will yield important insights that we do not have today and will not have if we stay on the same old, comfortable path.

ACKNOWLEDGMENTS

I am grateful to the editors for their helpful comments, thoughtful words of encouragement, and eye to creating an ever-larger audience for this work. I also wish to thank Ivar Berg, Harry Katz, Huseyin Leblebici, Daniel Levinthal and Harbir Singh for their invaluable insights into the organization and labor relationship framework and its implications.

REFERENCES

Allen, F. (1985) On the fixed nature of sharecropping contracts. *Economic Journal*, **95**, 30–48.

Allen, F. & Sherer, P. D. (1995) The design and redesign of organizational form? In B. M. Kogut & E. H. Bowman (Eds), *Redesigning the Firm*, pp. 183–196. New York: Oxford University Press.

Althauser, R. & Kalleberg, A. (1981) Firms, occupations and the structure of labor markets: A conceptual analysis. In I. Berg (Ed.), *Sociological Perspectives on Labor Markets*, pp. 119–151. New York: Academic Press.

Antilla, S. (1993) The latest free agents: Brokers. *New York Times*, 17 January, sect. 3, 15.

Barney, J. B. (1991) Firm resources and sustained competitive advantage. *Journal of Management*, **17**, 99–120.

Becker, G. S. (1975) *Human Capital* (2nd edn). Chicago: University of Chicago Press.

Cappelli, P. & Sherer, P. D. (1990) Assessing workers' attitudes under a two-tier wage system. *Industrial and Labor Relations Review*, **43**, 225–244.

Cappelli, P. & Sherer, P. D. (1991) The missing role of context in OB: The need for a meso-level approach. In L. L. Cummings and B. M. Staw (Eds), *Research in Organizational Behavior*, Vol. 13, pp. 55–110. Greenwich, CT: JAI Press.

Carlson, E. (1991) IRS takes hard line on independent contractor status. *Wall Street Journal*, 13 August, B2.

Cohen, W. M. & Levinthal, D. A. (1990) Absorptive capacity: A new perspective on learning and innovation. *Administrative Science Quarterly*, **35**, 128–152.

Davis-Blake, A. & Uzzi, B. (1993) Determinants of employment externalization: A study of temporary workers and independent contractors. *Administrative Science Quarterly*, **38**, 195–223.

DiMaggio, P. J. & Powell, W. W. (1983) The iron cage revisited: Institutional isomorphism and collective rationality in organizational fields. *American Sociological Review*, **48**, 147–160.

Doeringer, P. & Piore, M. J. (1971) *Internal Labor Markets and Manpower Analysis*. Lexington, MA: Health, Dore.

Eisenhardt, K. M. (1988) Agency- and institutional-theory explanations: The case of retail sales compensation. *Academy of Management Journal*, **31**, 488–511.

Fragin, S. (1994) Taxi. *Atlantic Monthly* (May), 30–34, & 42.

Galanter, M. & Palay, T. (1991) *Tournament of Lawyers*. Chicago: University of Chicago Press.

Gilbert, G. C. & Samuels, R. E. (1982) *The Taxicab*. Chapel Hill, NC: University of North Carolina Press.

Gilson, R. J. & Mnookin, R. H. (1988) Coming of age in a corporate law firm: The economics of associate career patterns. *Stanford Law Review*, **41**, 567–595.

Gorman, R. A. (1976) *Labor Law*. St Paul, MN: West Publishing.

Grant, R. M. (1991) The resource-based theory of competitive advantage: Implications for strategy formulation. *California Management Review*, **33**, 114–135.

Hogg, C. (1989) Executives for hire. *Director* (October), 134–136 & 138.

Johnston, D. C. (1995) IRS inquiry: Is IBM worker a contractor? *New York Times*, 6 July D3.

Klein, W. & Coffee, J. C. Jr (1990) *Business Organization and Finance: Legal and Economic Principles* (3rd edn). Westbury, NY: Foundation Press.

Machan, D. (1990) Rent-an-exec. *Fortune*, 22 January, 132 & 133.

Meyer, J. & Rowan, B. (1977) Institutionalized organizations: Formal structure as myth and ceremony. *American Journal of Sociology*, **83**, 340–363.

Milgrom, P. & Roberts, J. (1992) *Economics, Organization, and Management*. Englewood Cliffs, NJ: Prentice-Hall.

Morris, C. J. (1983) *The Developing Labor Law* (2nd edn) Washington, DC: Bureau of National Affairs.

Newberry, D. G. M. & Stiglitz, J. (1979) Sharecropping, risk sharing, and the importance of imperfect information. In J. A. Roumasset, J. M. Boussard and I. Singh (Eds), *Risk Uncertainty, and Agricultural Development*, pp. 311–339. New York: Agricultural Development Council.

Peterson, T. (1992) Payment systems and the structure of inequality: Conceptual issues and an analysis of salespersons in department stores. *American Journal of Sociology*, **98**, 67–104.

Pfeffer, J. & Baron, J. N. (1988) Taking the workers back out: Recent trends in the structuring of employment. In M. Staw and L. L. Cummings (Eds), *Research in Organizational Behavior*, Vol. 10, pp. 257–303. Greenwich, CT: JAI Press.

Phalon, R. (1993) How the bar girls beat the IRS. *Forbes*, 15 February, 136 & 137.

Rumelt, R. P. (1984) Towards a strategic theory of the firm. In R. B. Lamb (Ed.), *Competitive Strategic Management*, pp. 566–570. Englewood Cliffs, NJ: Prentice-Hall.

Rumelt, R. P. (1987) Theory, strategy, and entrepreneurship. In D. Teece (Ed.), *The Competitive Challenge: Strategies for Industrial Innovation and Renewal*, pp. 137–159. Cambridge, MA: Ballinger.

Russell, R. (1991) Sharing ownership in the services. In R. Russell and V. Rus (Eds), *International Handbook of Participation in Organizations*, Vol. 2, pp. 197–217. New York: Oxford University Press.

Salancik, G. & Leblebici, H. (1988) Variety and form in organizing transactions. In S. Bacharach (Ed.), *Research in the Sociology of Organizations*, vol. 6, pp. 1–31. Greenwich, CT: JAI Press.

Sappington, D. E. M. (1991) Incentives in principal–agent relationships. *Journal of Economic Perspectives*, **5**, 45–66.

Sells, W. E. (1975) *Agency*. Mineola, New York: Foundation Press.

Sherer, P. D. (1993) The variety in organization–labor relationships: A macro organizational and strategic framework to human resource management. Unpublished manuscript, The Wharton School, University of Pennsylvania.

Sherer, P. D. (1995) Leveraging human assets in law firms: Human capital structures and organizational capabilities. *Industrial and Labor Relations Review*, **48**, 671–691.

Sherer, P. D. & Lee, K. (1992) Cores, peripheries, and more and less: Mixes of labor relationships in firms. *Proceedings of the 1992 Industrial Relation Research Association*, pp. 317–324. Madison, WI: IRRA.

Sherer, P. D. & Lee, K. (1994) How are firms departing from employment relationships? Unpublished manuscript, The Wharton School, University of Pennsylvania.

Sherer, P. D. & Lee, K. (1995) Institutional or competitive versus strategic imitation: What better explains departures from standard HR practice in law firms? Unpublished manuscript, Johnson Graduate School of Management, Cornell University.

Sherer, P. D., Rogovsky, N. & Wright, N. (1995) What drives employment relationships in taxicab organizations? Linking agency to organizational capabilities and strategic opportunities. Unpublished manuscript, Johnson

Graduate School of Management, Cornell University.

Simon, H. (1951) A formal theory of the employment relationship. *Econometrica*, **19**, 293–305.

Steffen, R. T. (1977) *Agency-Partnership*. St Paul, MN: West Publishing.

Tolbert, P. S. & Zuker, L. G. (1983) Institutional sources of change in the formal structure of organizations: The diffusion of civil service reform, 1880–1935. *Administrative Science Quarterly*, **28**, 22–29.

Wagner, D. (1986) Variations on the "Of-Counsel" theme. *California Lawyer* (July), 59–62 & 64.

Wernerfelt, B. (1984) A resource-based view of the firm. *Strategic Management Journal*, **5**, 171–180.

Wholey, D. (1985) Determinants of firm internal labor markets in large law firms. *Administrative Science Quarterly*, **30**, 318–335.

Williamson, O. E. (1980) The organization of work: A comparative institutional assessment. *Journal of Economic Behavior and Organization*, **1**, 5–38.

Williamson, O. E. (1985) *The Economic Institutions of Capitalism*. New York: Free Press.

Williamson, O., Wachter, M. & Harris, J. (1975) Understanding the employment relation: The analysis of idiosyncratic exchange. *Bell Journal of Economics*, **6**, 250–278.

Wren, H. G. & Glascock, B. J. (1990) *The Of Counsel Agreement: A Guide for Law Firm and Practitioner*. Washington, DC: American Bar Association.

CHAPTER 7

The Expatriate Employee

Richard A. Guzzo

University of Maryland, USA

Some words, it seems, are in all vocabularies. "Business" is one. Of late, "global" seems to have become another. The globalization of business is a refrain repeatedly encountered as organizations have increased their activities abroad by competing in more markets, by locating production facilities overseas, by forming alliances with firms from other countries in the same industry.

As business in the global context has expanded, a number of specific aspects of management and operations in that context have drawn a great deal of attention. The one aspect this chapter focuses on is expatriate employment. Although the word "expatriate" may not yet have entered into as many vocabularies as have the words business and global, this grand old word carries a lot of meaning and implications. Expatriates, also known as international assignees (and sometimes as sojourners), are employees sent from a firm's home country to work in a foreign location. As the globalization of business has increased so has the importance of expatriate employees. This chapter examines some of the major developments regarding expatriate employees, including some of their unique circumstances and challenges as well as emerging issues for practice and research.

To be sure, expatriate employment is but one of many interrelated phenomena in the globalization of business. Other salient issues include such things as determining the right balance of influence and autonomy between a firm's headquarters and foreign establishments and effectively integrating different cultures into a single organization. Note that expatriate employees play a key role in each of these as representatives of the home office and as bearers of culture. While this chapter comes into contact with many strands in the bundle of issues that arise when a firm does business in other than its home country, the chapter's core

Trends in Organizational Behavior, Volume 3. Edited by C. L. Cooper and D. M. Rousseau
© 1996 John Wiley & Sons Ltd

interest is the individual employee working in an international context and the organizational practices affecting that employee. Also, this chapter mainly addresses issues of US employers and their expatriate employees, although the issues addressed are relevant to expatriates from countries other than the US.

Following a brief account of the characteristics of expatriate employment, this chapter addresses three broad areas of importance to expatriate work. They are *compensation, human capital*, and *well-being*. Expatriate compensation continues to be a sticky but key issue. The chapter briefly examines the status of expatriate compensation practices and addresses anticipated changes in how these practices are understood and implemented. Human capital considerations are addressed next. Two aspects of the human capital implications of international assignments are the developmental impact of overseas assignments on the employee and the employer's proficiency in getting the greatest value from their (current and former) expatriate employees. The next major section then addresses expatriate well-being. This topic subsumes a broad range of issues that center on the experiences of expatriate employees and their families. A brief conclusions section concludes the chapter.

These three topics—compensation, human capital, and well-being—are chosen for two reasons. The first is their importance to employee performance in an international assignment. Performance, for the purposes of this chapter, is defined broadly to include retention and on-the-job effectiveness, though the research literature has a more to say about retention than about on-the-job effectiveness. The second reason for choosing these three topics is that significant changes are underway in research and practice in these areas.

CHARACTERISTICS OF EXPATRIATE EMPLOYMENT

The prototypical expatriate employee of an American business organization is a person who leaves the corporate home office for an assignment of two to three years in a foreign country with the clear expectation of a return to the home country, if not the office from which the employee left. Many expatriates are managerial employees who go abroad with significant responsibilities, such as directing a production facility or a sales region or perhaps leading a business unit or foreign subsidiary of the home firm. Expatriate managers are almost always men, in their 40s, and 80% are accompanied by one or more family members (Guzzo, Noonan & Elron, 1994). There are many variations on this pattern, however, often related to industry. For example, firms in defense-related industries may send abroad technical specialists (e.g., aircraft maintenance personnel) and firms in energy industries may send abroad professionals (e.g., geologists). Overseas assignments may be of short duration, such as when pegged to a specific project (e.g., extinguish an oil well fire) or may extend through time, as when employees of the foreign services of governments spend the better part of their careers in foreign lands.

To a certain extent different circumstances of foreign assignments bring about different demands on employers and employees. Shorter-duration assignments have different implications than longer-duration assignments for the families of expatriate employees; the strangeness of dissimilar language and culture presents a very different situation than does a more familiar land. But one thing in common to all expatriate assignments is their expense. The direct costs of expatriate employees can be three to six times the costs of a comparable manager domestically (Freeman & Kane, 1995). There are many components to the cost of expatriate employees, including the costs of compensation, of relocating employee and family, of various expenses for employee and family (e.g., the costs of visits home), and the higher cost of living and doing business in certain countries. The costs of expatriate employment are a constant and significant source of pressure on firms and employees. Firms, of course, seek to minimize these costs, either by reducing the use of expatriates (Kobrin, 1988) or by changing the terms of expatriate assignments. For example, some companies have elected to send employees abroad for several intermittent short (e.g., one month) periods of time in an attempt to minimize the negative consequences of prolonged stays abroad and to avoid the costs of relocating employees' families overseas. But the costs of expatriate employment are not just the expenses incurred while an employee is abroad. Employees currently on international assignments who request an early return (i.e., before the planned term of working abroad is fulfilled) also represent significant costs when those requests are honored. Yet another costly aspect of expatriate employment is turnover. Turnover rates among expatriate employees appear to be high. For example, it is estimated that between 20% to 48% of repatriated employees intend to quit their employer within a year (Adler, 1986; Black, 1992; Handler, 1995). Further, the average costs of losing and replacing an expatriate employee substantially exceed those of the loss of the average domestic employee. Because of the expense and lost opportunity, the failure to retain expatriate employees is a substantial problem for employers. This chapter now turns to an examination of how compensation affects outcomes such as retention.

COMPENSATION

What is the "fair wage" for an employee in a foreign land? What financial inducements best secure the overseas service of a talented employee? To what extent need an employer protect expatriate employees from economic losses due to currency fluctuations and foreign taxation? These are some of the many issues germane to the compensation of expatriate employees.

Establishing appropriate (to employee and employer) direct compensation for expatriate employees continues to be a difficult issue but, considering all the factors involved, one that has become quite tractable. Employing organizations now have quick access to precise information, often available from vendors that rely on a network of associates who live in cities around the world, about the cost of living in almost any foreign location to which an employee might be sent. Information about the cost of living in a foreign land is contrasted to information about the cost of living in the home country to set employer policy through a "balance sheet" approach. This approach is predicated on the assumption that expatriates should live abroad much like they would live at home. A different approach is offered by Freeman and Kane (1995). Their "international citizen" approach would calculate compensation and benefit costs based on the cost of living in all countries to which an employer might send employees as well as employees' countries of origin. No matter how obtained, knowing in detail the current cost of housing, of transportation, of a basket of groceries and of other day-to-day expenses enables employers to devise a mix of salary, benefits, supplements (e.g., for housing), reimbursements, and other forms of compensation tailored to the particular employee and location of work.

Expatriate compensation is more complex than compensation for domestic employees for reasons beyond those of estimating equivalence of costs and payments among countries. One of the sources of complexity is the great latitude for employees to negotiate such things as deferments, bonuses, and other details when going abroad. Consequently, compensation arrangements are often quite unstandardized. This lack of standardization is one reason why expatriate employees, when encountering employees from other organizations, are said to be eager to "exchange notes". The absence of standardization also may contribute to perceived within-firm inequities in the pay of domestic versus overseas employees. Specifically, domestic employees often perceive their overseas peers as living an overpaid, exotic life. This lore has had some legitimacy in that some expatriates, especially early ones, indeed have accumulated wealth at a rate not possible had they remained at home. The opportunities to easily strike it rich by going overseas, however, appear to have diminished as employers become more exact in calibrating foreign to domestic compensation. On the other hand, more than a few expatriates have financially suffered by going abroad. Taxes, currency fluctuations, the failure to build equity through home ownership or through other investments, and unanticipated expenses are reasons why working overseas can be economically disadvantageous. The popular lore is relatively silent on the financial downside of working abroad. In summary, the compensation of expatriate employees is a complicated matter, surrounded by mixed experiences and perceptions, though the bases for determining compensation have become more explicit.

Compensation and Employer–Employee Relationships

An interesting finding from the study of expatriate managers reported by Guzzo, Noonan and Elron (1994) was that the amount of compensation did not, by itself, predict expatriates' attitudes and intentions to quit their employers. As the authors put it, "generous organizations . . . are not necessarily those that secure the strongest loyalty among their overseas managers" (Guzzo, Noonan & Elron, 1994, p. 622). What did predict expressions of organizational commitment and intentions to quit was the expatriates' evaluations of the extent to which their psychological contracts with their employers were fulfilled. Guzzo, Noonan and Elron argued that expatriate employees have very broad, expansive psychological contracts—subjective beliefs about what employers are obligated and expected to provide employees in exchange for their services—because expatriates' lives both on and off the job are greatly affected by their employers' practices. For example, the employer is not only a source of income but also is a source of support for expatriates' families through mechanisms such as assisting in finding schools for children and through practices such as paid-for trips home and domestic support for families living abroad. The broad terms of exchange between employer and expatriate employees include tangibles (e.g., pay) as well as intangibles (e.g., being treated with respect, being protected). As such, the expatriate employee comes to see the contract with their employer as a relational contract, one that concerns the totality of the relationship between employer and employee. Guzzo, Noonan and Elron's data indicated that as the fulfilment of the relational psychological contract increased expatriates' organizational commitment increased and their intent to quit decreased. Thus, the subjective evaluation of psychological contract fulfilment was more important as a predictor than the actual compensation and benefits received.

Looking Ahead

What does the future hold for research on and the practice of expatriate compensation? Compensation, broadly construed to include both direct payments as well as indirect supports and benefits for expatriate employees and their families, is crucial not only because it is at the core of the high costs of sending employees on foreign assignments but also because it is expected to affect employee retention and, presumably, effectiveness. As described above, the practice of compensation has evolved to a high level of sophistication regarding such things as establishing the equivalence of the cost of living in various foreign communities and finding benchmark data for things like subsidies for maintaining domestic homes while employees work abroad. It is the tangibles of the employer–employee exchange about which we have the most knowledge and certainty. In contrast, we know considerably less about the intangibles of the exchange for expatriate employees. If, as data suggest, the intangibles of the exchange between employer and employee are critical to understanding how expatriate employees assess their relationships with their firms—and thus influencing their loyalty and retention—then employers would stand to benefit by focusing their practices on managing those intangibles.

The psychological contract provides a useful conceptual handle here. That is, by understanding how expatriate employees evaluate the status (fulfilment, violation) of their psychological contracts key insights for practice can be obtained. By thinking in terms of psychological contract fulfilment, for example, a firm may learn that some of the most expensive forms of support it provides its expatriate employees may in fact have far less impact on an employee's evaluation of their psychological contract status than some less expensive supports. To illustrate, a firm may find that an expensive incentive premium (i.e., an inducement paid to an employee for accepting an international assignment) may have less impact than, say, the less expensive practice of providing a home fax machine and telephone line for the employee's family to stay in touch with friends and relatives at home. Focusing first on which of their possible practices most contribute to employees' positive evaluations of their relationship with the firm rather than focusing first on cost does not mean that a firm needs to abandon concern for the costs of those practices.

Two other points are worth noting. The first is that merely benchmarking what other firms do with respect to incentive premiums or fax lines or whatever does not provide information about how those practices affect employees' perceptions of the fulfilment of the psychological contracts. Such understanding comes instead from employees themselves (see Guzzo & Noonan, 1994, for ways of obtaining such information from employees). Benchmarking is useful but insufficient. Second, it would seem that flexibility and latitude in the compensation arrangements for expatriate employees remain valuable. Though such latitude creates practical burdens for those who oversee expatriate compensation in a firm, it also provides the opportunity for the employer to be responsive to the needs and preferences of international assignees on a case-by-case basis so as to generate loyalty and reduce expensive turnover.

Research on the psychological contract that both illuminates the nature of psychological contracts and ties itself closely to specific compensation practices for expatriates will be valuable for two reasons. One is that such research stands to contribute to the general understanding of employer–employee linkages and employee loyalty and turnover. Another is that such research has immediate applications to the practice of expatriate compensation. The results could be applied to the mutual benefit of employer and employee.

HUMAN CAPITAL

Human capital, broadly speaking, refers to the value of employees to a firm (Becker, 1993). The value of employees in human capital terms has two aspects, *firm-specific human capital* and *general human capital*. Firm-specific human capital refers to knowledge, skills, abilities, and experiences for which the value is specific to an employing organization. A professional baseball player's fielding and batting skills are examples of general human capital in that those skills are relevant to any baseball club. The rapport that a player has with the local fans is a form of firm-specific capital. Thus, Cal Ripken, Jr is a major league player of high repute who would bring a considerable amount of general human capital to any club that hired him. But to the Baltimore Orioles Ripken also has a great deal of firm-specific capital due to his family's connection to the organization, his longevity as a player in only the Orioles organization, and his being from the local area. In global firms general human capital comes from the innate talents of employees and from such things as MBA programs of study in which individuals acquire skills and knowledge that have value to and can be transported to any future employer. Firm-specific human capital is created through experience and accomplishment. A common attribute of firm-specific human capital in most businesses is that it comes in the form of intellectual attributes and products: facts, insight, judgment, wisdom, and know-how that are carried in the heads of employees. The competitive advantage of a company is enhanced through the creation of firm-specific capital.

From a firm's point of view, the management of expatriate employees often is an exercise in the development and management of firm-specific human capital. For example, expatriate employees can develop unique perspectives on the firm's operations and strategy as a result of doing business first-hand in a foreign land. Expatriates also develop different international professional networks and contacts compared to the domestic employee, contacts that could be quite useful in future business dealings. Expatriates also may develop knowledge about foreign markets that few or no other members of the organization have. There are many ways in which an international assignment could impart rather important firm-specific capital. While firm-specific competencies are being acquired, some more generalizable competencies also are likely to be acquired by expatriates, such as social skills that have potential future payoffs when working with members of a culture different from one's own. While both general and firm-specific human capital increase the value of the employee to the firm, it is the firm-specific aspects that carry the most value.

The process of managing expatriate human capital has two tracks. One concerns supporting the growth and development, through international assignments, of competencies and expertise in expatriate employees. The other concerns the utilization of acquired competencies and expertise during and especially after the completion of assignments.

Developing Human Capital Through International Assignments

Employee development is not always a goal of posting an employee in a foreign location but it is often a goal. The developmental value of foreign assignments is unambiguously recognized, for example, in those firms in which it is becoming expected that future managers at the most senior levels will have experienced one or more international assignments during their careers. Without such assignments managers may in fact be ineligible for promotion to the highest ranks. For the most part the developmental value of international assignments is assumed. But exactly what skills, knowledge, and abilities are in fact enhanced by overseas positions? What are the unique competencies imparted by international experience that are of the greatest value to the employer? Do skills and knowledge acquired while abroad actually contribute to improved performance in subsequent positions?

Little research to date on expatriates has examined these questions in detail. However, the documentation of the developmental value of overseas assignments is an important issue that appears to be on the verge of serious empirical inquiry, for several reasons. One is that the numbers of international assignees now makes this sort of research more likely. Another is that in recent years models of managerial and executive competencies have emerged that help pinpoint the kinds of modifiable skills and abilities essential to successful management. These models also bring with them tools and techniques for assessing those competencies, including 360° feedback instruments, business simulations, and other forms of assessment and learning. The opportunity to study the impact of international assignments on specific competencies and the long-term effects of such competencies on work performance is now at hand. Such research will make a significant contribution to knowledge about the growth and development of firm-specific human capital through international assignments and the products of this research will significantly shape the process of managing expatriates for maximal development.

Utilizing Human Capital Following International Assignments[1]

If what is widely assumed proves correct—that employees are enhanced by international assignments—then it is incumbent on the employing organization to take advantage of the knowledge, skills, and abilities uniquely gained by expatriate employees. Yet there is strong reason to believe that firms too often fail to do so. Rather than being able to retain and assign returned expatriates to positions that permit them to make the greatest use of their newly acquired competencies firms experience high rates of loss of such employees, as indicated in the earlier discussion of the intentions to quit expressed by repatriated employees. Considering that some part of the high cost of expatriate assignments constitutes an investment, high rates of turnover among repatriated employees represent a substantial loss of return on that investment as well as a rather sizeable depletion of human capital. Squandering money and losing human capital hardly serves the competitive advantage of the firm!

The loss of expatriates after their return to the home country appears to be closely tied to the more general issue of career management in organizations. Specifically, one of the most pervasive uncertainties among overseas employees is what job they will return to when their service abroad ends. Guzzo, Noonan and Elron (1993) found that among

---

[1] Naomi Dyer's work greatly influenced this section of the chapter.

expatriates' most frequently made suggestions for improving the experience of working abroad were suggestions that career planning be more explicit and better integrated with the international assignment. These data indicate that employers tend not to communicate what the nature of the subsequent assignment will be to expatriates and have not engaged in broader career planning with them. Poor career management practices prior to and during the period of expatriate work may be a prime cause of the high rate of loss of human capital following the completion of the international assignment. If overseas assignments are instrumental to career advancement in firms then those firms will need to engage in explicit and effective career management practices for their expatriate employees.

Looking Ahead

In fact, it appears that companies are becoming more active in managing the career aspects of expatriate work as evidenced by the growth in firms reporting career management practices. Almost no firms in the early 1980s reported engaging in career management practices for expatriates, a number that rose to nearly a third of US firms in the mid-1990s (Handler, 1995). Such programs are sure to vary greatly from firm to firm, and such variation presents an excellent opportunity for research. Some of the questions that most need research attention include: To what extent do career management programs reduce the turnover of expatriate employees? Which specific career management practices are most essential to the successful management of expatriates' careers after repatriation? To what extent do career management tactics change the experience of working abroad by reducing the uncertainty about future employment? What are the long-term consequences of career management practices for the employer?

Utilizing the human capital value imparted by international assignments requires not only the planning of careers but also the actual assignment of returning expatriates to the optimal positions for them. The optimal utilization of skills is an issue of concern to both employer and employee. Guzzo, Noonan and Elron (1993), to illustrate, reported evidence indicating that many expatriates feel that their employers do not appropriately make use of the value they have to offer when they return from an international assignment. To the extent this phenomenon is true it could result from a number of factors. For example, those responsible for determining the position to which overseas employees return may be unfamiliar with the positions from which they are returning and unfamiliar with expatriates as individuals, resulting in less-than-optimal assignments on return. Also, expatriates might be returning to a firm which has a future rather than immediate opportunity for calling on the recently acquired competencies of the former expatriate. Such a situation is not unreasonable from a firm's perspective but may frustrate the individual. Additional issues in need of research include identification of those factors that define the optimal person-to-job match for returned expatriates and better understanding of the experiences and encounters of the returned expatriate as they relate their performance in the positions to which they return. As globalization grows both the opportunity for and importance of research on the management of the valuable human capital embodied in expatriates rise.

EXPATRIATE WELL-BEING

For most, moving and working abroad is a profound experience. A different culture, community, perhaps language, and lifestyle are all part of that experience. The power of the experience is expressed in the reports of former expatriates who believe they were substantially changed as a consequence of working abroad (Osland, 1995). Because the experience can be so intense, there has always been an interest for the well-being of the employees who go overseas. For the most part, this interest has been expressed through the study of adjustment to a new culture and location.

Adjustment

Adjustment in international assignments has several dimensions. As Black, Mendenhall and Oddou (1991) describe, following a move to an international location adjustment can occur with respect to one's work, one's interaction with host country nationals, and with respect to the general environment (culture, lifestyle). Thus, it is theoretically possible that an expatriate could adjust well to work routines but have considerable difficulty adjusting to day-to-day living and leisure in the foreign land. The extent to which an individual expatriate employee successfully adjusts along any of these dimensions is thought to be a function of several factors. Some are controllable, such as the extent to which one has been prepared through predeparture cultural adjustment training, language training, and social support within the organization. Other influences on adaptation are beyond the control of employers and employees, such as the extent to which the foreign culture differs from the home culture (referred to as cultural "toughness" or "distance"). Parker and McEvoy (1993) examine the role of controllable and uncontrollable factors influencing expatriate adjustment. They find both to relate to adjustment.

According to Andersen (1994), traditional views of the adjustment process depict it in one of a few variations on a theme of orderly progression through time. One traditional view is that of a U-shaped curve of adjustment. In this account the expatriate experiences an initial "high" at the time of entry into the new culture, followed by a phase of steep reduction of well-being perhaps triggered by "culture shock", which is then followed by a rise to a healthy level of adaptation. Other traditional views of the process alternatively describe it as a learning curve in which adaptation increases rapidly at first and then gradually flattens or as a journey marked by increased self-insight and reduced ethnocentrism as the expatriate moves from the margins toward the center of the foreign culture. Andersen (1994) suggests that the dynamics of cultural adaptation are understandable as repeated expressions of frustration and accomplishment as newcomers to a culture solve problems and overcome obstacles. Although adaptation has several dimensions (work, interactions, environment) apparently there has been little attempt to link different processes of adaptation to the different dimensions.

Looking Ahead

Recent work on expatriate adjustment has begun to direct attention toward two related considerations. One is the role of the expatriate employee's family in shaping the employee's adjustment and adaptation to a new culture. The other is the role of social support. Family and social support appear to be emerging as key elements of the expatriate experience, elements that appear to have a bearing not only on expatriates' personal adaptation to new cultures but also on their ability to perform effectively in their work.

The well-being of the accompanying family as a predictor of the well-being and adjustment of the expatriate employee is explicitly noted by many, including Black, Mendenhall and Oddou (1991). Employers, however, differ considerably in the extent to which they provide for family members who accompany an employee abroad (Guzzo, Noonan & Elron, 1994). This is significant given the finding that, when asked to identify the best and worst aspects of the experience of living abroad, expatriate employees reported more unfavorable than favorable family-related experiences by a ratio of four to one (Guzzo, Noonan & Elron, 1993). Examples of unfavorable family-related experiences included children's adjustment problems, family stress, and difficulties related to spouses' careers. It would appear that firms could benefit from efforts to facilitate the transition of employees' families into a new culture by addressing these issues and by involving families in such things as predeparture training in cultural adaptation and language and providing local assistance to family members in the new culture.

Adelman (1988) provided one of the earliest accounts of the connections among expatriate adjustment, family, and social support. Adelman cites the importance of social support from one's close ties, such as family and friends, to adaptation. Interestingly, she also cites the importance of social support from weak ties or "fringe" relationships, such as one might have with locals who are shopkeepers, neighbors, or bartenders. Support from such non-intimate acquaintances in the local culture can be very instrumental to a sojourner to a new culture by providing explicit assistance in coping with daily life and by providing insights into the culture. These weak ties can be especially powerful early in the adaptation process, according to Adelman. Note that what is good for the individual expatriate employee is also good for the accompanying family members. Just as weak ties in the host community can be valuable to the expatriate employee such ties can be valuable to the employee's family. Weak ties might be of even greater value to the family since the family would not have the experience of the social contact that occurs in the workplace. The creation of weak ties, it would seem, is often within the realm of influence of the employer, such as when employers assist employees' families in finding stores and service providers in the local community.

Does family adjustment influence how well expatriates perform their jobs? Evidence answering this question directly is not abundant. However, Arthur and Bennett (1995) obtained opinions from 338 expatriates about factors that most contribute to effectiveness and success on international assignments. Five factors were identified, the most important of which was "family situation" (e.g., adaptability of spouse/family; stability of marriage). The other factors, in descending order of importance, were the personal flexibility of the international assignee, job knowledge and motivation, relational skills, and extra-cultural openness. Their findings further point to the potential utility of employer practices that enhance family adjustment abroad: not only does the family's adjustment appear to influence that of the employee but it also appears to influence the workplace effectiveness of the employee.

In summary, the role of social support for both expatriates and their families is a topic of emerging interest and importance. Especially interesting is the role of weak ties between members of the relocated family and members of their new local community. Employers may find it easy to facilitate the creation of weak ties. And the apparent consequences of social support—family adaptation and employee effectiveness—which are realized through both strong and weak ties are indeed outcomes of importance for all concerned.

CONCLUSION

The truly "global boundaryless firm" is a pipe dream. As long as countries exist businesses will always have a home country and peripheral locations. Consequently, there will always be expatriate employees sent from one country (culture) to another. Firms may be moving toward multiculturalism and greater worldwide integration but there will always be expatriates.

In this chapter three issues of long-term importance for expatriate employees were examined: compensation, human capital development and use, and employee well-being. These areas are characterized by emerging practices and research. These three, while not the only possible areas of interest, are interrelated rather than disconnected. For example, compensation practices, in the form of supports and benefits for families, can plausibly affect family well-being, which in turn can plausibly affect the use and retention of the human capital created through international assignments by enabling expatriate employees to perform well on the job and perhaps be more likely to remain with the firm following repatriation. The problems and prospects of expatriate work in the context of continued globalization make this an area with abundant opportunity for research. And that research has the good fortune of potentially accomplishing the rare feat of being at once novel, theoretical, and practical.

REFERENCES

Adelman, M. A. (1988) Cross-cultural adjustment: A theoretical perspective on social support. *International Journal of Intercultural Relations*, **12**, 183–204.

Adler, N. J. (1986) *International Dimensions of Organizational Behavior*. Boston: Kent.

Andersen, L. E. (1994) A new look at an old construct: Cross-cultural adaptation. *International Journal of Intercultural Relations*, **18**, 293–328.

Arthur, W. & Bennett, W. (1995) The international assignee: The relative importance of factors perceived to contribute to success. *Personnel Psychology*, **48**, 99–114.

Becker, G. S. (1993) *Human Capital* (3rd edn). Chicago: University of Chicago Press.

Black, J. S. (1992) Coming home: The relationship of expatriate expectations with the repatriation and adjustment and job performance. *Human Relations*, **45**, 177–192.

Black, J. S., Mendenhall, M. & Oddou, G. (1991) Toward a comprehensive model of international adjustment: An integration of multiple theoretical perspectives. *Academy of Management Review*, **16**, 291–317.

Freeman, K. A. & Kane, J. S. (1995) An alternative approach to expatriate allowances: An "international citizen". *The International Executive*, **37**, 245–259.

Guzzo, R. A. & Noonan, K. A. (1994) Human resource practices as communications and the psychological contract. *Human Resource Management*, **33**, 447–462.

Guzzo, R. A., Noonan, K. A. & Elron, E. (1993) Employer influence on the expatriate experience: Limits and implications for retention in overseas assignments. *Research in Personnel and Human Resources Management* (Suppl. 3), pp. 323–338. Greenwich, CT: JAI Press.

Guzzo, R. A., Noonan, K. A. & Elron, E. (1994) Expatriate managers and the psychological contract. *Journal of Applied Psychology*, **79**, 617–626.

Handler, C. A. (1995) Dual-career couples and career planning: Expatriate issues for the 1990s. Paper presented at the annual meeting of the Society for Industrial and Organizational Psychology, Orlando, FL.

Kobrin, S. J. (1988) Expatriate reduction and strategic control in American multinational corporations. *Human Resource Management*, **27**, 63–75.

Osland, J. S. (1995) *The Adventure of Working Abroad*. San Francisco: Jossey-Bass.

Parker, B. & McEvoy, G. M. (1993) Initial examination of a model of intercultural adjustment. *International Journal of Intercultural Relations*, **17**, 355–379.

CHAPTER 8

Renegotiating Psychological Contracts: Japanese Style

Motohiro Morishima*
Keio University, Fujisawa, Japan

INTRODUCTION

White-collar and managerial employees working for large Japanese corporations enjoyed a prolonged period of company growth and privileged employment status from the late 1950s through the 1980s. The pressures for individual contribution and company loyalty were intense as exemplified by the word *karoshi* (sudden death from overwork; Kawahito, 199). An implicit quid pro quo existed for the extreme dedication and personal sacrifice: a sense of entitlement to a good job and long-term employment security as long as an employee desired. Managerial workers usually enjoyed continuous salary growth, regular career promotions, and long-term employment security. Even the first severe recession to hit Japan in the 1970s, caused largely by the two oil crises in this period, did not destroy the practice of long-term employment for core, managerial employees in large Japanese firms (Rohlen, 1979).[1]

During this period, the most common Japanese contracts have been strongly oriented toward what Rousseau (1989) calls "relational" contracts, as opposed to what is called "transactional". Making an important distinction among the types of contracts that exist in organizations, Rousseau and her colleagues have advanced that psychological contracts (such as employment contracts) lie along a

---

[1] The current discussion is limited to core employees in large Japanese firms (usually defined as employment size larger than 1000). Employment contracts in the small-firm sector and/or for peripheral employees are argued to be qualitatively different (see Chalmers, 1989).

continuum ranging from the transactional, emphasizing limited time frames and economic benefit, to the relational, involving diffuse obligations for both parties and extended time frames (Rousseau, 1989; Rousseau & McLean Parks, 1993). Transactional contracts are characterized by exchanges of monetizable and pecuniary resources, short time frames for exchange completion, and delineation of specific obligations. In contrast, relational contracts are characterized by both pecuniary and non-pecuniary (e.g., socio-emotional) resources, indefinite duration for exchange completion and diffuse obligations. Another important characteristic of the transactional versus relational contract is that the former is often explicit and the latter is implicit, thus making the relational contract open to interpretation by the parties and subject to dynamic processes of change.

Indeed, employment contracts in Japan have had many of the important characteristics of relational contracts:

- Commitment and loyalty to organizations are emphasized
- Socializing with colleagues is often considered to be a required part of "work"
- The most common types of employment contracts are those that do not specify contract length
- Contract specifics are rarely spelled out, but assumed to be understood
- Contracts are rarely written down; verbally exchanged promises usually suffice
- Contracts are simply general agreements to work in good faith and fair dealing; specific obligations are to be filled on an ongoing basis
- Contracts are never taken to be fixed, but subject to continual renegotiation and reinterpretation by the parties

As many researchers have noted, these characteristics have given rise to the now famous Japanese work style in which employees are highly committed to their work and organization, flexible to accept any changes and continuously striving for improvement. The relational employment relationship that exists in Japanese organizations has successfully produced a workforce that has enabled Japan to become a major economic powerhouse. Although many other technological aspects of the employment relationship might also be responsible for this success, the nature of employment relationships and of psychological contracts between employers and employees has played an important role.

But the circumstances that helped create formal arrangements for managing core workers in large Japanese firms have changed. Companies, faced with slow growth, fierce domestic and international competition, bloated bureaucracies and high costs of human and capital investments, have resorted to a number of cost-cutting measures. An extremely strong yen and the bursting of the so called "bubble economy" of the late 1980s have also exacerbated Japanese employers' attacks on existing management practices, including their HRM practices. Most importantly, the type of continuous growth that has enabled firms to maintain long-term employment and stable career advancement for almost all employees has disappeared. Several remarked-upon trends are already emerging:

- White-collar and managerial employment insecurity due to employers' efforts to eliminate bloated white-collar ranks (Befu & Cernosia, 1990; Morishima, 1995c)
- Employers' heightened efforts to externalize their employment practices and use contingent employees (Morishima, 1995b)
- The rise of merit as opposed to seniority in the determination of career outcomes such as wages and promotions (Mroczkowski & Hanaoka, 1989; Morishima, 1992)
- Firms' increasing attempts to hire specialists from outside as opposed to training their own employees to be generalists (Nihon Keizai Shimbunsha, 1993)

Do these developments represent a significant shift in the nature of employment relationship that has existed over the last 40 years? This chapter proposes that these developments represent changes in such fundamental HRM practices as staffing, employee development, employment security, pay determination and performance standards. Since HRM practices are the signals through which employers communicate their intentions as to what is expected in the employment relationship, and the mechanism through which employees come to understand the terms of their employment contracts, changes in HRM practices have significant implications for the psychological contracts which employees come to perceive *vis-à-vis* their employers. If these changes are not managed properly, Japanese firms will be in danger of losing the psychological contract that has enabled them to develop and maintain a workforce that is highly committed both to existing organizational goals and to accepting to new challenges.

PSYCHOLOGICAL CONTRACTS IN JAPAN UP TO 1990

Psychological contracts refer to sets of beliefs and perceptions that individuals hold regarding the terms and conditions of a reciprocal exchange agreement. In employment relationships, employees' psychological contracts specify the contributions that they owe to their employer and the inducements and rewards that they believe are owed to them in return. The characteristics of these inducements and contributions define the type of psychological contracts that exist between employees and employers. In particular, psychological contract theorists have argued that among the many elements involved in defining the two types of psychological contracts, two dimensions appear to have the strongest discriminating power: the time horizon of contract duration and the specificity of transactions (Rousseau & Wade-Benzoni, 1994).

Time horizon refers to the expected duration of employment and ranges from limited term to unspecified long term. Specificity of transaction, in turn, refers to employees' and employers' understanding of what is to be exchanged in the employment contract. It ranges from an explicitly specified situation where employers expect specified performance standards to be met and employees expect to receive corresponding (mostly pecuniary) rewards, to the other end where employers simply expect dedication and loyalty from employees, and employees expect to receive such general outcomes as paternalistic treatment by employers. Along both of these dimensions, Japanese employment contracts have been relational.

Time Horizon

The duration of Japanese employment contracts is often unspecified and exchanges are assumed to be balanced over the unspecified, long span. When an employee is hired into the core workforce of a firm, he/she receives a contract which is implicitly open-ended and carries an implicit promise of employment guarantee until a point (such as the forced retirement age) where both parties agree to terminate the relationship (Koshiro, 1993). Thus, Japanese employment contracts are intended to be long term at the time of inception. The long-term nature of Japanese employment contracts (for core employees) is not an evolved outcome, but it is an intended outcome.

Two important consequences follow from this intended long-term nature of Japanese employment contracts. First, both employees and employers are expected to balance their exchanges over the course of an employee's entire career, a period which may cover, in many cases, more than 35 years. It is often speculated, as shown in Figure 8.1, that the relationship between contributions and inducements for a Japanese core worker is expected to balance over an employee's total tenure with an organization (see, for example, Shimada, 1994). In Zone a—b, employees

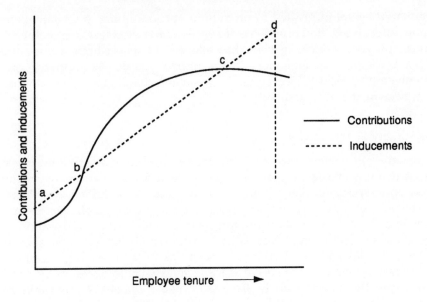

Figure 8.1   Long-term employment exchange in Japan
Source: Haruo Shimada (1994) *Employment in Japan.* Chikuma Publishing

whose firm-specific skills are yet to be developed are not capable of contributing to an organization fully. Yet, the organization pays them inducements that are higher than their contribution. Part of these inducements are paid in the form of training costs that are used to improve the value of an employee.

In Zone b–c, which covers the majority of an employee's tenure, an employee is expected, first, to pay for the higher-than-contribution inducements that firms paid in Zone a–b, and, second, to accumulate "loans" to the firm by working more than their inducements. Finally, in Zone c–d, Japanese employees, whose contributions tend to go down with the obsolescence of their skills, are expected to capture the returns of their loans to the firm, thus finally balancing the exchange relationship at the age of forced retirement (Point d). It is a planned process of balancing the inducements and contributions between employees and employers over a 35- to 40-year span.

The second consequence of the intended open-ended contract is that it enables firms to invest in long-term skill development of their employees. As noted by a number of researchers, one of the most important implications of long-term employment practices in Japan is their ability to encourage firms to invest in intra-firm training (Cole, 1992). Since employers are not likely to lose their investment in human capital, they are motivated to provide in-house training to their workers more intensively than otherwise. It has also promoted learning on the job by employees, which, in turn, has allowed Japanese firms to develop organizational technologies that utilize employee inputs and involvement, aspects represented by such technologies as continuous improvement and total quality control.

Specificity in Transaction

The other important aspect of the Japanese employment contract—at least as it now exists—is that reciprocal obligations are extremely general and underspecified. Since terms are only generally specified, details are to be worked out as time goes on and as circumstances change. Details are also subject to constant reinterpretation and further clarification as needs arise. On the employee, Ishida (1991) argues that concepts such as jobs and roles have very different meanings in Japanese organizations, since even when jobs are specified for individual employees, individuals are implicitly expected to "be flexible in their role behavior and take an "expansionist" view of [their] work" (p. 4). Extra-role behavior is a contractually built-in component of Japanese employees' behavior in which an employee is always expected to go beyond role requirements. Employees are expected to "contribute" to organizations even in the form of non-work behavior such as heavy socializing with colleagues after work and on holidays (Clark, 1979), thus blurring the boundaries between one's organizational role and other roles such as family member. Total inclusion of Japanese employees' lives into organizational settings has been well documented (see, for example, Clark, 1979).

Jobs in Japanese organizations are designed explicitly to take advantage of the organizational citizenship behavior that occurs as a consequence of relational contracts (Morishima, 1995b; McLean Park and Kidder, 1994). Research has shown that Japanese job classification is much simpler and broader, and that job assignments are much more fluid and flexible, compared to those in Western bureaucracies (Cole, 1979; Lincoln, Hanada & McBride, 1986; Aoki, 1988). Employees are expected to perform a wide range of job functions and accept frequent assignment changes as part of their regular day-to-day operations (Lincoln, Hanada & McBride, 1986). Relative to Western bureaucracies, individuals' roles have a lower degree of specialization and careers are structured around a general functional area or a product category, with specific assignments determined by the degree of employees' skill development and existing circumstances such as product demand. The lower degree of specialization in large Japanese firms has been reported in various case studies (Clark, 1979; Cole, 1979). A careful quantitative study conducted by Lincoln, Hanada and McBride (1986) also reports findings showing a lower degree of role specialization, relative to comparable US firms. According to the Ministry of Labour's [hereafter, MOL] survey of approximately 600 firms with an employment size of 30 or larger, only about 3 out of 10 firms (31.5%) agreed with the statement that "in our company, division of tasks and responsibilities are clearly specified for each job". In contrast, the responses from foreign-owned firms operating in Japan show that almost 6 out of 10 firms (59.5%) specify their division of labor clearly (MOL, 1993).

Thus, the combination of broadly defined jobs and psychological contracts that obligates employees to strive for organizational citizenship behavior enables Japanese firms to capture substantial returns from employee involvement and participation. Unlike the Western concepts of involvement and participation that emphasize motivational effects (Miller & Monge, 1986), the primary purpose of Japanese participation and involvement practices is to make effective use of the information and knowledge possessed by employees directly involved in the operation (Aoki, 1988). According to Aoki, participation increases firms' capabilities in problem solving and decision making by increasing the total amount of information that the organization can utilize. He conjectured that this aspect of Japanese management creates "information rent" which could be used to increase the value of the firm. Broadly defined jobs and participation in operational decision making also allows lower-level employees to introduce their own judgment into the work process and enables firms to capitalize on their relevant and concrete knowledge and information (Koike, 1988).

With regard to employer obligations, a generalized notion of "concern for employee welfare" is stressed (Dore, 1973). More specifically, three general principles are often stressed in the Japanese employment relationship as overall moral obligations that employers must fulfill (Lincoln & Kalleberg, 1990; Morishima, 1992):

(1) Employers take into consideration employees' welfare when making business decisions such as changes in HRM practices.
(2) Employers attempt to secure employment for their core workers even when that may not be the most "rational" decision from the efficiency perspective.
(3) Employers invest in skill development for their employees, which, in turn, raises the value (and compensation levels) of their employees.

Historically, these aspects of Japanese relational contracts were not something that had always existed in Japan, but an outcome of long (and often bitter) negotiations between employers and employees over the period since the end of World War II. In fact, the ten years after the end of World War II in 1945 marked an important era in the development of the basic elements of the current Japanese HRM/IR system. The most important of these elements was the formation and rapid diffusion of enterprise unions and their bargaining emphasis on the three principles of employer obligations. Up until the mid-1950s, the labor movement, often led by radical and militant unionists whose agenda centred around social revolution, frequently staged prolonged strikes. Work stoppages averaged 4.6 person-days lost per 10 employees per year in this period (Shimada, 1992). Bitter battles were mostly over protection of employee welfare and security and demands for employer investment in human resource development (Gordon, 1985). Assisted by the rapid growth of the economy throughout the 40-year period since then, Japanese employers have been able to maintain these principles at least for core workers in large firms.

DYNAMISM IN JAPANESE RELATIONAL CONTRACTS

Coupled with the open-ended nature of Japanese employment contracts, the process of mutual adjustment and constant modification becomes another salient and critical aspect of Japanese employment contracts. Since no specificity is usually included in the design of employment contracts, and only general terms of employment are offered instead, both employees and employers find it common that terms of employment contracts are constantly being renegotiated through changes in HRM practices (Morishima, 1992). In most cases, changes in employment practices are quite willingly accepted by employees when employers are perceived as showing a high level of concern for their welfare.

Then, an important question is what has made it possible for Japanese employers to attain a dynamic contract. Some even argue that the history of Japanese employment relationships over the last 40 years shows that Japanese employees have always engaged in constant reshaping of the terms of employment (Morishima, 1992; Rohlen, 1979). What made this dynamism possible? An answer lies in the dual structure of the Japanese psychological contract.

Table 8.1 shows that Japanese psychological contracts are exchanges of inducements and contributions on two levels. The first ("deeper") level is the basic agreement over the three principles of employer obligations and three corresponding employee obligations. The psychological contract at this level is similar to what economists call "trust" in the exchange relationship and is maintained by a strong assumption that neither party will violate the implicit terms of agreement (Barney, 1990).

Table 8.1 Structure of Japanese psychological contracts

	Employer side	Employee side
Surface level	Changes in HRM practices in response to circumstances	Acceptance of frequent changes in HRM practices
Deeper level	Concern for employee welfare	Acceptance of organizational goals
	Long-term employment security	Avoidance of short-term maximization of labor market opportunities
	Investment in human capital development	Application of acquired skills for the benefit of employer

When violated, however, the total system becomes unstable and no further exchanges are possible without immediate fulfilment of obligations. The relationship quickly becomes transactional.

As long as stability in the deeper level is maintained, however, psychological contracts between employees and employers can be extremely fluid at the second ("surface") level. Term of exchanges, inducements and contributions can change without difficult negotiations between the parties or major violations of contracts. It is at this level where Japanese employers have been able to obtain a substantial amount of freedom and flexibility in changing their employment terms and HRM practices as circumstances have demanded, a phenomenon Dore (1986) calls "flexible rigidities".

One good example is the introduction of *shukko* in the recessions of the 1970s in which employees agreed to be transferred to subsidiaries and other related firms in order to maintain employment. Since subsidiaries and related firms may have different HRM practices from those in the parent firm, it is a violation (or at least a change) in employment contract at the surface level. The implicit promise of continuous employment is kept, however, thus avoiding a violation at the deeper level. The dynamism that is associated with the psychological contract between Japanese employers and employees has been predicated on the maintenance of the relational contract at the deeper level. Morishima's (1992) evidence also shows that many changes in HRM practices are quite willingly accepted by employees when employers are perceived as upholding the three principles of "trust" between employees and employers by showing concern for employee welfare, practising employment stabilization policies, and investing in skill development.

CHANGES IN JAPANESE HRM PRACTICES

Two aspects are most important in Japanese employers' recent efforts to modify their employment practices: the introduction of pay-for-performance schemes and the introduction of externalized employment arrangements within the firm workforce. Some of the recent changes that are occurring in Japanese HRM practices, however, are likely to threaten the basis of trust between Japanese employers and employees.

Introduction of Pay- and Promotion-for-Performance

There is currently an increasing move toward more competitive appraisal and reward practices, more specifically, toward pay- and promotion-for-performance schemes for white-collar employees. This move is most visible in the compensation arrangements for middle and senior managers, although a number of firms have also tried to introduce management-by-objectives (MBO) for their non-managerial white-collar employees.

While Japan built its economic powerhouse on blue-collar productivity through such mechanisms as the lean production system, its white-collar productivity has lagged behind Western nations by, according to some estimates, more than 50% (Hori, 1993). According to a 1992 study by the Japan Productivity Center [hereafter, JPC], in white-collar dominated industries such as banking and finance, and wholesale and retail, Japanese productivity is two-thirds to three-quarters of that observed in the United States and 80–90% of that in Germany and the United Kingdom (JPC, 1992). In contrast, the JPC study shows, in the auto manufacturing and electrical appliance industries—two industries where Japanese manufacturing has been globally competitive—Japanese productivity levels are very similar to those observed in the US and Germany. Also, in the most carefully conducted study of white-collar productivity differences to date, Hori (1993) estimates that in wholesale and retail, a Japanese firm with an average level of productivity needs to improve its productivity by more than 20% to be competitive with comparable US firms in the same industry.

The reason for the low productivity levels among white-collar employees is, in part, due to the lack of appropriate performance measurement schemes in Japanese white-collar HRM. As noted earlier, the Japanese model of HRM is premised on the assumption that firms recruit candidates with the largest learning potential, provide them with continuous training opportunities, and reward them according to the degree to which they have acquired internally relevant job-related skills. Yet, since learning takes on such an important meaning, performance itself and the task of measuring it are often neglected (Nonaka, 1988). The elaborate skill-grade system which is used to assess employee development often ends up being used to assess performance. More importantly, since compensation based on the level of learning is also likely to be relatively stable, it does not reflect fluctuations in the levels of employees' actual contributions to the organization.

During the past 40 years, this system has been successful because of the relative stability in the firm environment and consequently in firm strategies. This type of learning-based assessment and reward system is suitable when the goals of an organization are more or less constant and the type and contents of skills related to achieving these goals are relatively known. Organizations can then prepare a set of increasingly complex tasks on the learning table and teach employees these skills in an incremental manner. The assumed link between learning content and behavioral requirement did not have to be questioned.

Up to the late 1980s, almost all white-collar managers and administrative employees were paid on the basis of their skill levels. Consequently, there was very little variation in managers' pay from year to year. This began to change in the early 1990s when many firms proposed to eliminate the seniority component in senior managers' pay. Firms began to introduce reward arrangements based on individuals' performance levels.

Most notably, MBO practices began to be introduced for middle and senior managers. According to a 1993 RECRUIT survey (N = 319), 46.4% of large firms reported using some type of MBO practice, with 67.5% of larger firms (employment >3000; N = 123) using the practices (RECRUIT, 1993). A JPC survey conducted in 1993 indicates that of the firms using MBO practices for managers, 10.1% determine all managerial pay changes (increases and decreases) on the basis of goal attainment (JPC, 1994). Given that this practice was not even discussed in previous surveys such as MOL (1987), these numbers must be considered substantial.

For example, Fujitsu, the second largest computer manufacturer in the world, put all of it 6000 middle and senior managers on strict MBO compensation as of 1 April 1993, where up to 30% of their annual pay could be variable depending on their performance assessment. Since the idea of MBO-type compensation was so foreign to managers, Fujitsu had a trial period of six months prior to full-scale introduction and prepared a 15-page booklet explaining the system. Fujitsu is planning to introduce MBO-style compensation to its non-managerial white-collar administrative workforce and computer hardware and software engineering employees within the next year. At Hino Truck Manufacturing, an MBO system is being introduced for all its 200 managers, whose annual pay may vary up to 50%, depending on their performance.

In most cases, these changes also involve a shift in the kinds of goals that employers negotiate. The JPC survey indicates that of the firms that have adopted MBO practices, 86% attach at least 50% of the weight to goals that are specific to individual managers. Moreover, the use of individually specified goals increases when MBO practices are targeted to senior level managers. For the highest managers at the divisional level, almost 100% of the firms attach all the weight to individual goals.

All Nippon Airways (ANA), Japan's second largest passenger carrier put all of its 6800 white-collar administrative and technical employees on MBO, including those not in management positions. The uniqueness of ANA's MBO system, however, is that for white-collar employees with relatively short tenure (fewer than 9 years), skill development goals are specifically designed into the goal-setting process. In this sense, for junior employees, ANA's model represents a transitional model from the skill-grade system to more performance-oriented practices.

Use of Externalized Employment Arrangements

Externalization of employment has been proceeding in a similar manner in Japan (Morishima, 1995b) as has been the case in the US (Pfeffer & Baron, 1988) and other countries (Thurman & Trah, 1990). As noted by Morishima (1995a), however, one of the important motivations for Japanese firms to engage in externalization practices is to respond to the constraints imposed by highly structured internal labor market practices. More specifically, Morishima (1995b) argued that Japanese firms (and, theoretically speaking, firms in other countries) create multiple contractual arrangements within their firms' labor force in pursuit of multiple human resource goals. These multiple goals could include such outcomes as flexibility of human resource deployment, cost control, skill enhancement, and employee commitment maximization. Therefore, through the increased use of contingent employees (part-timers and temporaries), for example, firms may pursue goals of cost control and deployment flexibility, while maintaining other outcomes such as skill enhancement and commitment maximization in their permanent, regular-status workers. Morishima's (1995b) evidence, based on a sample of medium-size food service establishments, shows clearly that establishments that engage in strong internal labor market practices (e.g., intensive internal training, reward for long service, and payment of above-market wages) for their regular-status workers have a larger proportion of contingent workers.

Similar arguments were made for the general expansion of externalized employment in US firms (Pfeffer & Baron, 1988). Due to Japan's highly structured internal labor markets, however, firms have had limited choices in their attempts to increase their employment flexibility and control labor cost. The result has been the proliferation of multiple contractual arrangements coexisting in the firm workforce, all designed to create segments of the firm workforce associated with weaker employment protection than previously assumed for the regular-status workers (Nihon Keizai Shimbunsha, 1993). Japanese firms have begun to externalize their employment not only through use of part-timers and temporaries, but also by hiring limited-contract employees and sorting (based on performance and potential) employees into segments with different levels of employment security. A variety of new programs are also being devised to remove senior white-collar employees from the permanent payroll.

For example, Nitto Denko, a manufacturer of industrial equipment, announced in June 1993 that it will sort its white-collar employees, after four years of tenure, into those who will advance in some specialty and those who will advance in general management. At Sumitomo Rubber, new results are expected to be designated, at the time of hiring, to one of two career tracks similar to those used at Nitto Denko, on the basis of management judgment and employee preference. In Japanese firms, specialist positions have usually carried weaker employment protection than those making progress through the management hierarchy. In both cases, the firms' intention is to identify those who will have weaker employment security very early in their tenure.

In sum, changes in Japanese employment practices are occurring in two areas: first, in the shift of appraisal and reward criteria from those based on ability progression and seniority to performance and career potential and, second, in the decrease in the proportion of core employees protected by strong employment security. Since these changes started to be discussed most seriously in the early 1990s, the psychological impact of these changes on employees' perceptions of their psychological contract and, consequently, on their behavior have not been examined empirically.

PSYCHOLOGICAL IMPACTS OF CHANGES IN EMPLOYMENT PRACTICES: A SPECULATION

Japanese employees are increasingly evaluated on the basis of specific role behavior (performance) instead of generalized commitment to the company. Similarly, employers are changing the expected length of the employment relationship from open-ended, long-term employment to more specified, limited-term contracts. The changes in these two areas are moving employment contracts in Japan from those closer to the relational end to those closer to the transactional end. The implications of this shift can be discussed from two perspectives:

(1) Renegotiation of psychological contracts.
(2) Violation of psychological contracts.

Renegotiation of Psychological Contracts

Changes in HRM practices in Japanese firms are likely to continue in the future, and so is the renegotiation of psychological contracts between employees and employers. These developments will continue, however, without too much impact on either employers or employees *as long as* the psychological contract regarding the support and concern for employee welfare is kept intact and the principles of employment such as the three discussed earlier (see Table 8.1) are maintained.

However, renegotiations even at this surface level will have an important implication for the effectiveness of Japanese job design and consequently, the effectiveness of organizational structure based on employee participation and involvement. In Japanese organizations, even a slight movement from the relational end in psychological contracts and a shift in employee behavior will have detrimental impacts on organizational effectiveness since jobs and organizations are designed explicitly to take advantage of employees' active role "making". Thus, to the extent that a move to a more performance-oriented appraisal and reward scheme and employment externalization convinces employees that employers' obligations have changed and, therefore, that their obligations must also change, the effectiveness of the organizational and job design which has been successful for the last four decades may be undermined. The match between employment practices and organizational design will be lost since employees will no longer see that their ties to their employing organizations will be based on relational contracts. Very little change has been observed in job design in Japan, and there are indications that roles are becoming even more broadly defined due to the flattening of hierarchical structures (Nihon Keizai Shimbunsha, 1993). How Japanese firms reconcile the move toward more transactional psychological contracts and the continued and expanded use of broadly defined jobs will determine the continued effectiveness of Japanese organizations.

On the employee side, there are unique concerns associated with these changes in companies' HRM practices. Making the transition from school to a good job will become more difficult for individuals as employers are more inclined to use externalized employment arrangements. Once in a job, employees will have much greater responsibility for managing their own careers—identifying and achieving performance goals that will get them opportunities for advancement and being aware of employment opportunities outside the company. One of the most important consequences of these changes is that Japanese employees now face greater risks in compensation and in the development of their careers.

The concept of loyalty and commitment will also change from the traditional sense of long-term behavioral attachment to firms to more short-term attachment to work projects and goals. Perhaps the word "involvement" better represents the new ways through which employees relate to their firms. Employees are involved in projects and goals that will bring them visible, short-term results and are less committed and loyal to organizations per se. They will rely less on the long-term balance of exchanges with their employers, and seek short-term settlements of their accounts.

Violation of Psychological Contract

A major threat is likely, however, when psychological contracts are broken at a deeper level where principles of employment such as those noted earlier are eliminated, especially unilaterally by employers. This situation may, however, occur because:

(1) Japanese stockholders, who had been resigned to the fact that their investment was there to provide stable capital for the firm and would not yield returns except in the form of long-term (in the order of 30 to 50 years) company growth, have come to demand higher dividends and, more importantly, quicker return on their investments. These developments will put pressure on Japanese managers to take short-term economic efficiency into consideration in making their decisions. If this continues, investment in human capital and employee well-being, which will produce results only on a long-term basis, will be replaced by short-term cost-cutting measures which may violate the basic rule of concern for employee welfare, employment security and skill development.

(2) The emphasis on performance may evolve to the extent of firms trading externally purchasable skills for internally developed human resources. Performance is a function of skills/abilities and motivation, and whether an organization acquires motivation and skills externally through market-mediated methods, or through the development of internal labor market structures is a choice often influenced by rational calculations as well as by managerial values. Managerial values may be slower to change (see Morishima, 1995c), but there is a point where value preferences will be overridden by economic considerations. Especially as performance standards become clearer and more specific and employee

contributions are measured in terms of tangible outcomes, it becomes easier for firms to trade long-term development for market-transacted motivation and skills. Here again, the principles of long-term employment skill development may be discarded.

(3) The increased use of externalized employment practices, while restricted to enhancing the protection and development of core workers to this point, may proceed to the extent of entirely removing the core workforce. Virtual corporations and an all contingent workforce are still quite foreign in Japan, but the demarcation between core and contingent have been blurred to the extent that the same tasks are often carried out by both core and contingent employees. Especially in workplaces where innovation and creativity often depend on the infusion of new ideas (e.g., research and development labs), it has become quite common to use contingent workers, not as a supplementary workforce, but as a replacement for the core workforce (Nihon Keizai Shimbunsha, 1993).

Working side by side with the contingent (and yet critically placed) workers heightens core employees' awareness that the boundary between themselves and contingents has got thinner and the buffering of their employment conditions from those of contingents is no longer impermeable. The psychological contract of attachment to the firm in exchange for protection of employment and concern and support for employee welfare will also be threatened.

Thus, there are reasons which indicate the current changes in HRM practices may undermine the basic principles that have given the Japanese employment system both stability and flexibility. What will happen if these principles are completely eliminated is a question that is yet to be examined. But two scenarios are possible:

(1) Japanese employers will abandon all three principles and attempt to renegotiate the entire psychological contract at both levels.

This scenario is not likely since these changes will damage the flexible rigidities in the Japanese psychological contract which has imparted to the Japanese economy high levels of resilience in times of economic recession. Abandoning these principles will also make employers susceptible to changes in bargaining power. In times of economic downturn and slack labor markets, employers' bargaining power is stronger, and employers are likely to be able to initiate and reap the gains from changes in employment relationships. However, if employers violate the principles of the psychological contract that has held the employment system together for the last 40 years, an improvement of the economy and tightening of labor markets may well lead to a very different situation where employee turnover escalates rapidly and wages follow as employers scramble to retain key individuals. Even the medium-term commitment necessary for work structures such as self-managing teams and workplace participation may be lost because of the extremely short-term orientation of employees who are simply reacting to employers' violation of the deep-rooted principles of the psychological contact.

(2) Employers renegotiate a subset of the principles, but not all.

A more likely scenario is that Japanese employers will attempt to renegotiate a subset of the principles, but not all, thus preserving some of the characteristics of the traditional system. Which principles will Japanese employers attempt to modify? Logic and empirical evidence (Morishima, 1995c) indicate that most Japanese employers will preserve the long-term, open-ended nature of their employment relationship and will shift to short-term, specific performance standards (such as those used in MBO) in evaluating and rewarding employees.

Logically, the combination of specific performance standards and open-ended contract duration gives employees the security to develop their skills and opportunities to make contributions with little risk-bearing, but at the same time, allows organizations to take account of employee contributions on a relatively regular basis without relying on loyalty and commitment. Rousseau and Wade-Benzoni (1994) also advocate this type of psychological contract as "balanced" and argue that it is effective for team-oriented, involvement-based work structures.

Empirically, Morishima's (1995c) evidence indicates that out of the 1168 firms he surveyed, only about 10% show both substantial weakening of employment security *and* assessment based on specific performance standards. The rest of the firms were almost evenly divided into those which have both long-term employment security *and* long-term development-based assessment ("traditional firms"), and those which have long-term employment security and assessment based on specific performance standards ("transformed firms"). Japanese firms, if they attempt to fundamentally renegotiate their psychological contracts with their employees, appear to opt for a "balanced" psychological contract.

Employment contracts are changing not only in Japan but also in the US (McLean Parks & Kidder, 1994) and other countries (Hunter, McGregor, MacInnes & Sproull, 1993). With the use of "balanced" contracts, however, firms in Japan as well as in other countries should be able both to impart more "flexible rigidities" to their employment relationships and to take advantage of new work structures based on employee involvement and team arrangements.

ACKNOWLEDGMENT

The author thanks Nancy Bartter and Denise Rousseau for their comments on previous drafts.

REFERENCES

Aoki, M. (1988) *Information, Incentives, and Bargaining in the Japanese Economy.* New York: Cambridge University Press.

Barney, J. (1990) The debate between traditional management theory and organizational economics: Substantive differences or intergroup conflict? *Academy of Management Review*, **15**, 382–393.

Befu, H. & Cernosia, C. (1990) Demise of "permanent employment" in Japan. *Human Resource Management*, **29**, 231–250.

Chalmers, N. J. (1989) *Industrial Relations in Japan: The Peripheral Workforce.* London: Routledge.

Clark, R. C. (1979) *The Japanese Company.* New Haven, CT: Yale University Press.

Cole, R. E. (1979) *Work, Mobility, and Participation: A Comparative Study of American and Japanese Industry.* Berkeley, CA: University of California Press.

Cole, R. E. (1992) Issues in skill formation in Japanese approaches to automation. In P. S. Adler (Ed.), *Technology and the Future of Work*, pp. 187–209. New York: Oxford University Press.

Dore, R. P. (1973) *British Factory, Japanese Factory: The Origins of National Diversity in Industrial Relations.* Berkeley, CA: University of California Press.

Dore, R. P. (1986) *Flexible Rigidities: Industrial Policy and Structural Adjustment in the Japanese Economy, 1970–80.* London: Athlone Press.

Gordon, A. (1985) *The Evolution of Labor Relations in Japan: Heavy Industry, 1853–1955.* Cambridge, MA: Harvard East Asian Monographs.

Hori, S. (1993) Fixing Japan's white-collar economy: A personal view. *Harvard Business Review* (November–December), 157–172.

Hunter, L., McGregor, A., MacInnes, J. & Sproull, A. (1993) The "flexible firm": Strategy and segmentation. *British Journal of Industrial Relations*, **31**, 383–407.

Ishida, H. (1991) *Flexibility in Japanese Management.* Presented at the Workshop on Labor in Japan—An Approach to Labor-Management Cooperation. Manila, Philippines, 1 February.

Japan Productivity Center (1992) *International Comparison of Labor Productivity.* Tokyo: Japan Productivity Center (in Japanese).

Japan Productivity Center (1994) *Survey Report on the Future of the Lifetime Employment System.* Tokyo: Japan Productivity Center (in Japanese).

Kawahito, H. (1991) Death and the corporate warrior. *Japan Quarterly*, **38**, 149–157.

Koike, K. (1988) *Understanding Industrial Relations in Modern Japan.* London: Macmillan.

Koshiro, K. (1993) *Comment on "Aging Population and Human Resource Management" by M. Ito.* Presented at Japan Institute of Labour–University of Illinois Institute of Labor and Industrial Relations Conference on "The Change of Employment Environment and Human Resource Management in the U.S. and Japanese Labor Markets". Tokyo, 5 October.

Lincoln, J. R., Hanada, M. & McBride, K. (1986) Organizational structure in Japanese and US manufacturing. *Administrative Science Quarterly*, **31**, 338–364.

Lincoln, J. R. & Kalleberg, A. L. (1990) *Culture, Control and Commitment: A Study of Work Organization and Work Attitudes in the United States and Japan*. New York: Cambridge University Press.

McLean Parks, J. & Kidder, D. L. (1994) "Till death us do part . . ." Changing work relationships in the 1990s. In C. L. Cooper & D. M. Rousseau (Eds), *Trends in Organizational Behavior*, vol. 1, pp. 111–136. New York: John Wiley.

Miller, K. I. & Monge, P. R. (1986) Participation, satisfaction, and productivity: A meta-analytic review. *Academy of Management Journal*, **29**, 727–753.

Ministry of Labour (1987) *Prospects on Changes in Japanese Employment Practices: Survey Report*. Tokyo: Ministry of Finance Printing Office (in Japanese).

Ministry of Labour (1993) *1993 White Paper on Labour*. Tokyo: Japan Institute of Labour (in Japanese).

Morishima, M. (1992) Japanese employees' attitudes toward changes in traditional employment practices. *Industrial Relations*, **31**, 433–454.

Morishima, M. (1995a) The Japanese human resource management system: A learning bureaucracy. In J. D. Jennings and L. Moore (Eds), *HRM in the Pacific Rim: Institutions, Practices, and Values*, pp. 119–150. Berlin and New York: Walter de Gruyter.

Morishima, M. (1995b) Externalization of Employment as a Response to Internal Labor Market Constraints. Manuscript under review.

Morishima, M. (1995c) *The Evolution of HRM Policies and Practices in Japan*. In D. Lewin, D. Sockell & B. Kaufman (Eds), *Advances in Industrial Labor Relations*, vol. 7. Greenwich, CT: JAI Press (forthcoming).

Mroczkowski, T. & Hanaoka, M. (1989) Continuity and change in Japanese management. *California Management Review*, **31**, 39–53.

Nihon Keizai Shimbunsha (Ed.) (1993) *Japanese-Type Personnel Management is No More*. Tokyo: Nihon Keizai Shimbunsha (in Japanese).

Nonaka, I. (1988) Self-renewal of the Japanese firm and the human resource strategy. *Human Resource Management*, **27**, 45–62.

Pfeffer, J. & Baron, J. N. (1988) Taking the workers back out. In B. M. Staw and L. L. Cummings (Eds), *Research in Organizational Behavior*, vol. 10, pp. 257–303. Greenwich, CT: JAI Press.

RECRUIT (1993) *A Survey on Japanese Personnel Systems and Employee Development*. Tokyo: RECRUIT Co. (in Japanese).

Rohlen, T. P. (1979) Permanent employment faces recession, slow growth, and an aging workforce. *Journal of Japanese Studies*, **5**, 235–272.

Rousseau, D. M. (1989) Psychological and implied contracts in organizations. *Employee Responsibilities and Rights Journal*, **2**, 121–139.

Rousseau, D. M. & McLean Parks, J. (1993) The contracts of individuals and organizations. In L. L. Cummings & B. M. Staw (Eds), *Research in Organizational Behavior*, vol. 15, pp. 1–43. Greenwich, CT: JAI Press.

Rousseau, D. M. & Wade-Benzoni, K. A. (1994) Linking strategy and human resource practices: How employee and customer contracts are created. *Human Resource Management*, **33**, 463–489.

Shimada, H. (1992) Japan's industrial culture and labor-management relations. In S. Kumon & H. Rosovsky (Eds), *The Political Economy of Japan, vol. 3: Cultural and Social Dynamics*, pp. 267–291. Stanford, CA: Stanford University Press.

Shimada, H. (1994) *Employment in Japan*. Tokyo: Chikuma Publishing (in Japanese).

Thurman, J. E. & Trah, G. (1990) Part-time work in international perspective. *International Labour Review*, **129,** 23–40.

CHAPTER 9

Social Networks and the Liability of Newness for Managers

David Krackhardt
Carnegie Mellon University, Pittsburgh, USA

INTRODUCTION

In his classic piece on organization theory, Stinchcombe (1965) suggested that organizations could be better understood by taking into account the "social structure" in which they find themselves. By "social structure" he meant the broad set of societal variables that remained fairly stable over time and which had a bearing on the life of the organization. In the course of reviewing this broad set of environmental conditions, he noted that young organizations tended to suffer a premature demise (relative to seasoned organizations). This was especially true for organizations that required a new "form", a new way of organizing. He cited four reasons (Stinchcombe, 1965, pp. 148–149) for this "liability of newness":

(1) "New organizations . . . involve new roles, which have to be learned". Old organizations can draw on the experience of their members to deal with the varieties of specific problems, exceptions, and disruptions to routines. New organizations must rely on the generalized experiences of their numbers, experiences that may not be as relevant to the current organization's problems. Thus, there is a *learning curve disadvantage* suffered by new organizations.
(2) The process of inventing and developing new roles has "high costs in time, worry, conflict and temporary inefficiency". That is, the organizational learning creates its own side effects that themselves are

Trends in Organizational Behavior, Volume 3. Edited by C. L. Cooper and D. M. Rousseau
© 1996 John Wiley & Sons Ltd

costly for the new organization. These side effects may be thought of as *process disadvantages*.

(3) "New organizations must rely heavily on social relations among *strangers*" [emphasis mine]. In particular, Stinchcombe notes, the critical relationship of "trust" is more difficult to obtain when people do not have the history together to be able to predict what colleagues will do in response to any given situation or information (Karckhardt, 1994). Thus, new organizations suffer from a *trust disadvantage* relative to established firms.

(4) Much of the work of an organization, in terms of its inputs from suppliers and outputs to customers, transpires through well-established relationships among those sets of organizations. Customers provide repeat business in part because they are familiar with how the focal organization works, how it handles different orders, and consequently how to get exactly what they need. Familiarity with how the organization fits into the larger system of organizational transactions is a distinct advantage for the older, experienced organization. A new organization, then, suffers from a *systems knowledge disadvantage*, knowledge of how the system of exchanges works around them and how it fits comfortably and profitably into this system.

While Stinchcombe eloquently argued for this phenomenon at the organizational level, it is apparent that the same rationale can be applied to managers who emerge in a new organizational environment, either through hiring or through transfer. In today's world, the rapidly changing technology, the restructuring and downsizing of organizations, and the general mobility of the population make this problem even more salient. Managers frequently find themselves in the unfamiliar territory of new organizations or new organizational subunits. Such managers carry with them role expectations from their prior positions, roles that may not be compatible with the expectations of colleagues within the new organizational unit. It takes time to learn these expectations; thus, managers new to the specific organization experience their own kind of learning curve disadvantage. Collaterally, in the process of learning, changing and experimenting, they are likely to create anxiety and conflict among others in the organization. Moreover, since trust inherently takes time to build (Krackhardt, 1994; Mayer, Davis & Schoorman, 1995), the new manager will often wait before introducing substantial changes that require sincere trust among herself and her new peers, subordinates and superordinates (Gabarro, 1987).

But perhaps the most critical liability to the new manager is the lack of a clear understanding of how the current system of exchanges and relationships works in the organizational unit. Just as within the macro system of organizations, these relationships are often subtle, not explicit, not formally declared or even admitted to by the participants. That makes them difficult for the newcomer to observe. An established hand, who perhaps rose up through the internal ranks of the organizational unit, has learned this web of ropes through years of experience. The newcomer must try to sail in these unchartered waters without so much as the occasional blink of a dim lighthouse to guide him.

Thus, managers new to an organizational unit suffer from many of the same disadvantages attributed to new organizations. Before they can operate effectively in this new environment, they must get a good handle on how things are accomplished (Krackhardt, 1990). Before they can change the organization, they must know who is likely to benefit, who is likely to resist, and who is likely to support either the beneficiaries or the resisters (Krackhardt, 1992).

These limitations are given. They are the common experience of all managers who have not come through direct promotions from below (Gabarro, 1987). The question I intend to address in this paper is how the new manager can survive this inherent liability of newness. In particular, I would like to show how the new manager can use social network analysis to overcome this liability.

SOCIAL NETWORK ANALYSIS AS A DIAGNOSTIC TOOL

New managers, whether they are transferred or hired from the outside, often are selected because they had success in dealing with similar managerial problems in other contexts. But, their success often involved understanding how their context actually worked. They knew whom they could count on, who the coalitions were, what positions they would likely take, and which battles they could win and which ones were better left unfought. If they introduced change, they would likely know who would accept it, who would fight it, and how to manage that resistance.

While such are keys to successful change management, this knowledge is specific to the context in which the manager is operating. It takes time to find out who the key actors are and what positions and actions they are likely to take. Such political knowledge, however, is essential if the manager is to accomplish anything more than maintain the status quo.

Social network analysis has been used primarily as an analytic technique for academic organizational researchers (Wasserman & Galaskiewicz, 1994; Krackhardt & Brass, 1994; Mizruchi & Galaskiewicz, 1994). While some attention has been paid to how managing extant networks can be profitable for the manager (Baker, 1994), very little has been written on how these powerful techniques can be used to diagnose organizational problems.

To this end, I will present two cases wherein a new manager, faced with "liability of newness" problems, was enabled with network analysis to diagnose and successfully introduce organizational changes. The first case illustrates how simply knowing the social network can help the manager identify who the important political players are. The second case illustrates how network analysis can identify the problem itself as well as who must be involved in the solution.

THE CASE OF THE TRANSFERRED AUDIT MANAGER

The firm, Halifax,[1] was a large defense contractor on the west coast. One division of Halifax, the aircraft engine manufacturing division, had several plants that were subject to an extensive auditing routine to comply with federal mandates. The group of interest here is the internal auditing staff of this division, composed of 14 employees. They had fallen behind in their auditing schedules, and top management expressed some concern that this could jeopardize Halifax's relationship with the Department of Defense, upon whom Halifax depended for more than half its business.

Normally, management vacancies in Halifax were filled, to the extent possible, by promoting from within the units. This policy kept morale high and drew on the knowledge and experience of those within those units. But, when Bob Kramer, the manager of this auditing unit, chose to move on, Sheila Jackson, the Comptroller of Halifax, decided that his successor should not come from within the local unit because she was afraid that this would perpetuate the problems that this unit was experiencing. Instead, she selected a successful auditing manager, Manuel, from another manufacturing division. Manuel had been instrumental in reorganizing the auditing group where he currently worked, the results of which had decreased turnover and increased auditing output without adding to the staff.

Manuel assumed his new assignment with considerable confidence. As he saw it, the problems the aircraft auditing group faced were similar to those in his prior auditing group, and most of these problems stemmed from a lack of coordination between the auditors and the secretarial staff.

The work of this auditing group was fairly routine. Audit teams of one to three auditors would visit a manufacturing plant, often spending up to a weak at the site collecting and cross-checking the financial records.

---

[1] All names and other specific identifying remarks in this paper are disguised to protect the anonymity of the site.

The auditors would return home with a satchel full of forms and supporting working papers. These papers were then given to the supervisor of the wordprocessing center (Donna), who in turn assigned the task of processing the forms to one of the four members of the secretarial pool. After the forms were processed, the finished product was returned to the auditor.

The formal organizational chart for this group is provided in Figure 9.1. The four managers are represented by ellipses; the staff auditors are represented by diamonds; and the secretaries are in boxes. Stuart and Charles, the two audit supervisors, often accompanied the auditing groups to the sites. Each audit team (teams were recomposed for each audit) had a leader who was responsible for getting the forms to Donna in a timely manner. Once the audit forms were in Donna's hands, the turnaround time was under the control of the secretarial pool.

Manuel's first task was to find out why the audits were taking an inordinate amount of time (the average audit was taking 28% longer than comparable audits in other parts of Halifax). He interviewed each supervisor and each auditor individually and the secretaries as a group. From these interviews and from audit records on file, he determined several things. First, morale among the staff was not a particular problem. Kramer had been a low-key manager, protecting his group from the eventual criticisms that would emerge from higher in the organization. For the most part, everyone was doing their part with diligence, if not efficiency.

Second, he determined that while most auditors were completing their visits to sites in a timely manner, certain exceptions could be explained by particularly difficult circumstances at the site. Where audits seemed to take somewhat longer for no apparent reason, he found that the

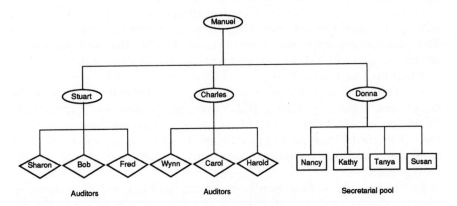

Figure 9.1 Formal organizational chart for auditing group

auditors had had little idea that their performance had been lacking. From their perspective, the audits were completed on schedule.

In reality, the majority of the delays came from a lack of coordination with the secretarial pool. Audits papers that should only take an afternoon to be processed would occasionally take several days. Several audits would come in at once, stretching the resources of the pool. Some of the secretaries were more efficient than others, and the slower ones would occasionally require the help of the more experienced ones, when they had time. Donna managed this process as best she could, but much of the coordination was managed informally by the secretaries themselves.

Manuel decided to put into effect some organizational changes that he had used when he was promoted in his prior assignment, changes that had been quite successful. First, he instituted an immediate feedback system, so that the auditors knew how much time the audit actually took relative to how long it was projected to take. Second, he reorganized how the auditors and secretaries worked together. The most visible change he made was that he reassigned the secretaries to work directly for an individual auditor. He assigned the most experienced secretaries to the auditors who typically did the most difficult audits (including Charles and Stuart), and the less experienced secretaries were assigned to auditors who typically handled routine audits. He also instituted a scheduling system that took into account when each secretary would likely get a set of papers to process, so that secretaries would not be suddenly overwhelmed by too many audits at once. Donna retained her title as supervisor, but her responsibilities changed considerably. She no longer assigned secretaries to audits; instead, she acted as a facilitator when problems arose and she spent more of her time assisting the other secretaries when they fell behind or needed help.

Manuel announced his new organization plans at a group meeting with all his staff present, including the four secretaries. There was very little discussion; everyone seemed content with the new operation, which Manuel labeled an "experiment" to try to deal with the delays that had occurred in the past.

The first week of the new organization was difficult for some of the secretaries, especially Tanya and Susan, who were less experienced. Manuel made clear that the auditors would not expect more from them than they could be expected to deliver, and by the second week there were few audible complaints emanating from any corner of the workgroup.

By the end of the first month, however, backlogs were beginning to mount. Eleven audits had been performed, which was exactly the number Manuel had scheduled, but the processing among the secretaries, even with Donna's extra help, was not meeting the demand. Manuel was concerned, because he could not discern any particular source of the overall problem. The secretaries were each competent and apparently motivated, but somehow the work was encountering glitches, which had accumulated into a total of a week's backlog of paperwork.

Manuel considered hiring some additional staff to help with the workload. But he knew this would not be received well by the corporate office. He approached me to ask my advice on how he should handle this problem. In our first meeting, Manuel outlined the problem, his attempted solution, and the disappointing results. I responded by saying that it appeared to me that the problem was not in the plan but in the implementation. I proposed a simple network study of the group to help identify possible centers of support or resistance to his organizational changes.

I administered a questionnaire to all 14 members of the group. In the questionnaire, I asked one simple question: Who among the other 13 people here in the auditing group do you typically go to for help or advice when you encounter a problem or have a question at work? I also asked the converse question: Who typically comes to you for help or advice when they have a question or a problem at work? They were instructed to select as many of the 13 people as were appropriate in response to the question. All 14 employees (including Manuel) completed the questionnaire.

The responses were collapsed into a picture (see Figure 9.2). The answers to the network questions were represented by lines and arrows between the names. For example, the arrow going from Donna to Manuel meant that both Donna and Manuel agreed that Donna typically went to Manuel for help and advice at work. A double-headed arrow, such as found between Stuart and Charles, meant that both parties agreed that they each typically went to the other for help and advice. Over the years, I have found that these pictures communicate much more than any number of statistical results (Krackhardt, Lundberg & O'Rourke, 1993; Krackhardt, Blythe & McGrath, 1994). The picture was drawn so that the arrows tended to point upward on the page, revealing an informal status hierarchy. Those higher on the page where the recipient of advice requests, those lower on the page were the ones going to others for advice, those in the middle were both giving and getting advice (see McGrath, Blythe & Krackhardt, 1995, for a description of how different drawings of the same network can communicate different information).

The picture itself showed that many people went to the supervisors for help and advice, and that these informal advice relations by and large stayed within their particular work subgroup (secretaries went to

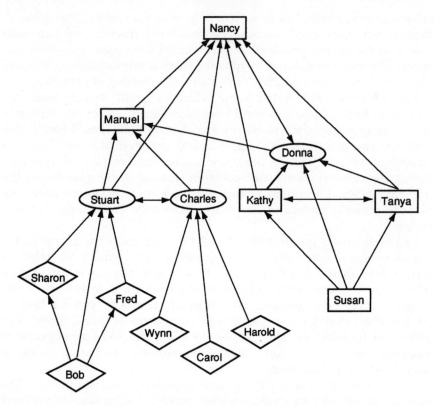

Figure 9.2   Advice[a] networks for auditing group

[a] A line from A to B indicates that A goes to B for help or advice at work

secretaries, auditors went to auditors within their subgroup). But, there was one notable exception to this pattern. Nancy, one of the two experienced secretaries, was the recipient of an inordinate number of advice lines. In fact, she was at the top of the page, indicating the highest informal status. Moreover, Nancy was approached both by secretaries and by experienced auditors. Even Manuel went to Nancy for help and advice.

Almost immediately upon seeing this picture of the advice network, Manuel slapped his hand to his forehead and exclaimed, "Of course! I forgot to ask Nancy!" I was not sure what Manuel meant by this remark, so Manual explained.

> I knew Nancy before I even came to this unit. I have always respected her uncanny ability to forecast both audit problems and problem audits. She knows what rules have to be obeyed and which ones can be bent. What I

didn't realize before I saw this picture was how much the rest of this group relied on her also. I should have thought of it, but it just didn't occur to me.

What also occurred to Manuel was that if Nancy was not behind the changes he was making, she could subtly, even unconsciously, make it difficult for these changes to succeed.

Manuel decided to approach Nancy directly. He asked her in private what she thought of his decision to break up the secretarial pool, and she replied after some prodding that she thought it was not a good idea (her reasons for this were not articulated, but Manuel sensed that she felt a loss of autonomy when she was assigned to two of the auditors). Manuel then asked her what she thought would help to improve the coordination problem between the auditors and the secretaries. She was not forthcoming with any ideas, but she promised to think about it.

Manuel decided to reconstitute the secretarial pool. Over the next two months, he worked with Nancy to device a compromise solution to the problem, wherein auditors were temporarily assigned secretaries for particular auditors, and wherein the secretaries (especially Nancy) had a say in what those assignments were going to be. By the end of the third month, the aircraft auditing group had improved its performance considerably, with the audits beating the standard time allotted by an average of 10%.

THE CASE OF THE INSURANCE COMPANY CRISIS

This case differs from the prior case on several dimensions. One important factor was that the network data were collected not in response to a managerial problem but rather as part of a larger research project. Coincidentally, the data were useful to one incoming manager, as I will describe later.

Allway Insurance Company (AIC) is a large, East Coast firm that specializes in hazard insurance. They have assets in excess of several billion dollars. AIC enjoys a reputation as having one of the most successful and lucrative financial investment strategies in the industry. This success was amplified during the fast growth financial times of the 1980s.

One consequence of this success was that internal control of some expenses was lax. As one principal in the firm put it,

> We were making so much money and growing so fast that we didn't care about these incidental expenses. They were small potatoes. We figured it wasn't worth reining them in because it would take precious time and energy away from our ever-growing investment opportunities.

After the 1987 market crash, there was less room for such glib oversight. The firm's overall performance started to decline. Top management started taking a harder look at expenses in the company. What they found was disturbing, especially in the MIS division.

The MIS division was a core group of computer experts who handled all information systems hardware and software requirements for the various users in the firm. There were three types of users: administrators, who wanted an MIS system that allowed them to access large personnel and internal accounting databases on demand; sales people, who wanted an MIS system that easily generated options and forms for customers to buy and sign; and financial asset managers (investors), who wanted the state-of-the-art high-powered MIS systems that allowed them to have immediate access to stock, bond and options trading, as well as sophisticated modeling capabilities for market forecasting. Each group asked for (and received) a completely different system, tailored to their own desires. The financial asset managers themselves demanded several, often expensive, workstations from a variety of manufacturers, which employed different and incompatible operating systems. To make matters worse, the investors were demanding hardware upgrades almost continually to keep up with the fast-paced technologies.

The MIS group was responsible for ordering, installing, and connecting these systems. Moreover, they were responsible for ordering, installing, connecting and disconnecting phone and ethernet lines as people moved from one floor to the next. One of the disturbing facts that top management discovered in their detailed examination of expenses in the firm was that as people moved and requested new phone lines, their old phone lines were not being disconnected. By 1990, the firm was paying for over 2000 phone lines that were not being used. To make matters worse, the MIS group seemed overworked and were not getting their orders completed to the satisfaction of various user groups, especially the investors.

The technical problems of multiple, incompatible systems and dead phone lines were clear and solvable, but unfortunately they were only the most obvious of a host of problems that the MIS group faced, including the growing dissatisfaction among users. The more disturbing question to top management was, how was it possible that things were allowed to get this out of hand?

Clearly, drastic changes were needed. The AIC executive committee decided to hire an MIS expert from outside the firm to revamp the MIS division and its role in the firm. Steve Russell was hired from AT&T. Russell had had more than 10 years of operational experience at IBM before he had become director of information services to one of AT&T's large divisions. He knew the technology, he knew how information systems worked in large diverse organizations. He appeared to be the right person for this job.

Russell spent his first three months figuring out how AIC worked, what its IS needs were, and where its organizational weaknesses might be. He acted quickly to reduce some major obvious costs. For example, he ordered all phone lines disconnected that did not have a recent record of activity. As he anticipated, this resulted in a handful of irate users who found one of their phone lines disconnected. He reconnected this small number of lines and mollified these users (including one executive committee member) by convincing them the drastic step was necessary to get a handle on the problem.

By the end of the third month, Russell felt he had managed to cut back on many of the wasteful practices of the unit. He had personally addressed and solved many specific problems. But, he still faced the more difficult question of figuring out how to set up a system so that such problems did not get out of hand in the future. Russell was baffled by the fact that the problems had got so severe without anyone realizing it and without anyone within the unit being able to do anything about it.

He had spoken both to users and to all his staff in this unit. He concluded that the problem was not one of personnel; the MIS unit was made up of dedicated and competent people. Also, the current organizational structure (see Figure 9.3) made sense to him. There were four groups, three specializing in particular IS technologies (one hardware, one local area networks, and one software), and one "User Support Group", made up of people who were both facile with the various technologies and good at interfacing with users. Users mainly had contact with the User Support Group, and these people knew how much they knew and when they had to rely on the more detailed

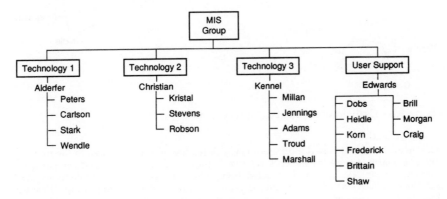

Figure 9.3

expertise provided within the various technology groups. Russell had developed a similar system at AT&T, and it had been quite successful. He was not sure why it was not working here at AIC.

It was after Russell's second month that I had scheduled to collect some network data in his unit. In this case, I asked the 25 employees of the MIS group to check the names of all those who they talked to virtually every day about work-related matters.[2] The answers are depicted in Figure 9.4. A line between two people in the figure indicates that they both agreed that they talked to each other virtually every day.

One difference between this study and the prior case at Halifax is that at Halifax, the manager (Manuel) had approached me to help him out. In the current case, Russell had not contacted me. My access came from another part of the organization. Russell, in fact, was skeptical. He tolerated my data collection and agreed to participate in a feedback session, but he considered himself too busy to be bothered by a research project that was

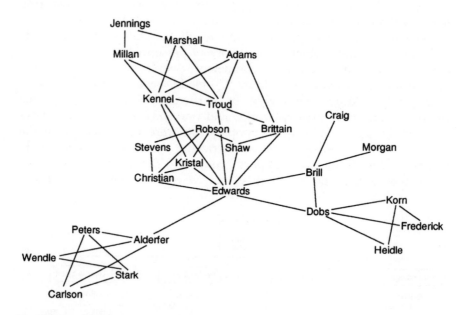

Figure 9.4 Daily interaction at insurance company

---

[2]One might note that I used a different network relation in this case than in the previous one. I regularly change the network relation I study to fit the context and the particular problems of the site. In fact, I collected information on six different relations for AIC, including an "advice" relation similar to the one I used at the auditing group. However, this simple "interaction" relation was the one that proved most informative for Russell, so that is the only one I am reporting here.

clearly academic in flavor. While he was curious, he foresaw little application in what I was doing to the problems he was facing.

At the feedback session, I presented a series of network pictures on several different relations. When I put up the network in Figure 9.4, he stared in disbelief.

"That's it!" he said. I had no idea what he was talking about, since I did not know what the "it" was. Subsequently, in a series of interviews with Russell and several of the employees in the MIS group, I discovered what he had seen in that figure.

Russell had had in his mind the way work should be coordinated within his MIS group. Users would contact someone in the User's Support Group and make a request, that person would facilitate the interaction between the relevant technology group(s) and the request would be filled. The support people would be translators, facilitators, and would do much of the installation work themselves. That was Russell's understanding of how it worked, and that is how it worked at AT&T.

When he realized when he saw the picture was that Edwards, head of the User Support Group, was doing all the coordinating. Edwards was talking to the technology people and to two key assistants in his User Support Group. All requests were going through Edwards, he was deciding which technology groups to involve and which experts to connect up with which users and/or support people. Edwards was a good people-manager, and he had good technical skills, which enabled him to have the confidence of his fellow workers to take on this central role. But, Edwards was obviously not delegating. He was overwhelmed with work, with decisions. Everyone was busy, so no one minded that he took on that coordinating role. Nor did anyone notice that Edwards was the source of huge backlogs and even lost information.

In contrast to this, Russell had imagined that all the User Support Group would have easy and equal access to the relevant technology experts. He had not expected Edwards to occupy such a central role, not to the exclusion of all others, anyway. Edwards was a bottleneck to the organization's ability to respond in a timely fashion to the fast changing demands posed by information technology.

The formal organizational chart (Figure 9.3) only communicated formal relationships, not how work was actually performed in the organization (Krackhardt & Hanson, 1993). The form chart was similar to the formal chart he had used at AT&T, and he had consequently assumed that the work was channeled in much the same way. What the network picture confirmed for him was that work was not being accomplished as he thought it should.

Russell valued Edwards' contribution to the team effort. He did not want to jeopardize Edwards' enthusiasm by demoting him. However, it became clear that Edwards himself thought that he was in over his head and would welcome some relief from the pressure of his daily activities. So, Russell completely reorganized the unit, redefining the functions of the technology groups to focus on products rather than parts. In addition, he split up the User Support Group, assigning its members to different product groups. While it was not his stated intention, his reorganization and redefinition of job titles had the effect of turning the group into a flexible, proactive team of problem solvers, rather than a mechanized, centralized group of problem reactors.

Russell was not committed to this structure in the long run, but it broke the logjam created inadvertently by Edwards in his former position. Within a year, user complaints were down considerably, and costs were contained. Russell reorganized again at that point to solidify the changes he had made and better match the formal structure with the demands of the firm.

DISCUSSION

In both these studies, the network did not solve the problem faced by the new manager. In both cases, I, as the one who collected and analyzed the data for the manager, could not infer from the network pictures how to solve their particular problems. There are no general solutions to problems based on such pictures alone. They provide insight; but only when such insight is accompanied by a local sense of the problems and dynamics can these network pictures be useful.

Having said that, though, the new manager can be a particular beneficiary of such pictures. In Stinchcombe's model, the liability of newness is based on organizational learning. The young organization suffers from being inexperienced in the new environment and from being higher on the learning curve; it suffers from the tension and other costs of the changes it often has to make to survive; it suffers from not enjoying the trust accrued by older established firms; it suffers from a general lack of knowledge of how the web of transactions and relationships works.

New managers suffer similarly. Manuel suffered from not enjoying complete trust from his subordinates. While the network picture did not establish that trust for him, it did inform him where he had to invest his energies to get trust so that the others would follow suit. Russell suffered from a lack of understanding of how work was accomplished in his MIS group. The network picture did not tell him how work was accomplished directly. Rather, he knew that if work was being accomplished in the way he thought it should, then the informal network would not look like the way it did. Plus it gave him enough of a clue about how work was being channeled through Edwards that he was able to quickly confirm this suspicion and fix the problem. Understanding the social network of an organization can be a very efficient way for new managers to overcome the "liability of newness".

In closing, I am reminded of Kurt Lewin's famous dictum: If you want to understand an organization, change it. I would offer a variation on that dictum: If you want to change an organization, understand it. Pictures of critical networks in the organization can facilitate that understanding and enhance the probability that the new manager will survive.

REFERENCES

Baker, W. E. (1994) *Networking Smart*. New York: McGraw-Hill.

Gabarro, J. (1987) *The Dynamics of Taking Charge*. Cambridge, MA: Harvard Business School Press.

Krackhardt, D. (1990) Assessing the political landscape: Structure, cognition, and power in organizations. *Administrative Science Quarterly*, **35**, 342–369.

Krackhardt, D. (1992) The strength of strong ties: The importance of philos in organizations. In N. Nohria & R. Eccles (Eds), *Networks and Organizations: Structure, Form, and Action*, pp. 216–239. Boston, MA: Harvard Business School Press.

Krackhardt, D. (1994) Constraints on the interactive organization as an ideal type. In C. Heckscher & A. Donnellan (Eds), *The Post-Bureaucratic Organization*, pp. 211–222. Beverly Hills, CA: Sage.

Krackhardt, D., Blythe, J. & McGrath, C. (1994) KrackPlot 3.0: An improved network drawing program. *Connections*, **17**, 53–55.

Krackhardt, D. & Brass, D. (1994) Intra-organizational networks: The micro side. In *Advances in the Social and Behavioral Sciences from Social Network Analysis*, pp. 209–230. Beverly Hills, CA: Sage.

Krackhardt, D. & Hanson, J. (1993) Informal networks: The company behind the chart. *Harvard Business Review*, **71** (4), 104–111.

Krackhardt, D., Lundberg, M. & O'Rourke, L. (1993) KrackPlot: A picture's worth a thousand words. *Connections*, **16**, 37–47.

Mayer, R. C., Davis, J. H. & Schoorman, F. D. (1995) An integrative model of organizational trust. *Academy of Management Review*, **20**, 709–734.

McGrath, C., Blythe, J. & Krackhardt, D. (1995) The effect of spatial arrangement on judgments and errors in interpreting graphs. *The Heinz School* Working paper.

Mizruchi, M. S. & Galaskiewicz, J. (1994) Networks of interorganizational relations. In S. Wasserman & J. Galaskiewicz (Eds), *Advances in Social Network Analysis: Research in the Social and Behavioral Sciences*, pp. 230–253. Thousand Oaks, CA: Sage.

Stinchcombe, A. L. (1965) Social structure and organizations. In J. G. March (Ed.), *Handbook of Organizations*, pp. 142–193. Chicago: Rand McNally.

Wasserman, S. & Galaskiewicz, J. (1994) *Advances in Social Network Analysis*. Thousand Oaks, CA: Sage.

Index

Index compiled by Liz Granger.

Existing volumes in the Trends in Organizational Behavior Series...

Series Editors: **CARY L. COOPER** and **DENISE ROUSSEAU**

Volume 1 - Contents

- Functional and Dysfunctional Organizational Linkages
- Meso Organizational Behavior: Avoiding Three Fundamental Biases
- Coordinating Global Companies: The Effects of Electronic Communication, Organizational Commitment and a Multi-Cultural Managerial Workforce
- The Human Effects of Mergers and Acquisitions
- Work and Family: In Search of More Effective Workplace Interventions
- Personality and Personnel Selection
- The Psychological Contract as an Explanatory Framework in the Employment Relationship
- 'Till Death Us Do Part...": Changing Work Relationships in the 1990s

Volume 2 - Contents

- Occupational Stress Management: Current Status and Future Directions
- Effective Implementation of Organizational Change: An Organizational Justice Perspective
- Applications of Groupware in Organizational Learning
- The Impact of Job Relocation: Future Research
- Entrepreneurship in East Europe: A General Model and Empirical Findings
- Diagnostic Models for Organizations: Toward an Integrative Perspective
- Employees at Risk: Contingent Work and the Psychological Experience of Contingent Workers
- Cross-Cultural Issues in Organizational Behavior

All volumes are available to purchase from John Wiley & Sons Ltd, Baffins Lane, Chichester, West Sussex, PO19 1UD, or alternatively, subscribe to the **Journal of Organizational Behavior** to receive volumes in this annual series as part of your subscription!

Related titles of interest from Wiley...

Handbook of Work and Health Psychology

Edited by **MARC J. SCHABRACQ, JACQUES A.M. WINNUBST,** and **CARY L. COOPER**

The Handbook covers the concepts and problems which define the field, the diagnosis of individual stress and psychological work hazards, interventions and methods for a wide range of specific problems, and, finally, preventive programs for health promotion and counseling at work. Process problems of career development and organizational change are covered, as are acute problems like burnout and alcohol or drug misuse, and the special problems of women at work and the impact of new technology are also addressed.

0-471-95789-5   504pp   1996   Hardback

Handbook of Work Group Psychology

Edited by **MICHAEL A. WEST**

This volume offers a comprehensive and authoritative overview of empirical research on groups at work. It covers a number of subsections, including the *contexts of work groups* such as group structure and group tasks; *group processes* including minority dissent, psychodynamic phenomena, decision-making, leadership, autonomy; *group outcomes* including effectiveness, innovation and mental health; *groups in organizations* which deal with commitment, intergroup relations, work group socialization, and communication; *cultural differences in group processes; interventions in work groups;* and a concluding chapter which offers conceptual integration.

0-471-95790-9   632pp   1996   Hardback

International Review of Industrial and Organizational Psychology

Edited by **Cary L. Cooper** and **Ivan T. Robertson**

This series of annual volumes provides authoritative reviews in the field of industrial and organizational psychology. Includes chapters on important existing and new topics in the organizational psychology field.

ISSN: 0886-1528   Annual   Available on subscription